THE GOLD DIGGER'S CONFESSION

Nancy Panoch

Publisher: Expert Subjects, LLC

The Gold Digger's Confession
An Expert Subjects' book, published by
agreement with the author
Copyright 2015 © Nancy Panoch

ISBN: 978-1-68074-002-8
Printed in the United States of America

Cover Design by Jason Alexander at www.expertsubjects.com

Expert Subjects, LLC

DEDICATION

When my eight year old granddaughter, Gabriella, was visiting my beauty salon, sitting under the hair dryer with rollers in her hair, she was searching to find her Daddy's name in my first book, "Accountable The Joseph Usher Story." Upon finding his name she questioned me why her name was not in the book. I promised her that her name would be in my next one.

So, Gabby Sudah, this book is dedicated to you and the Panoch brothers, Kendrick, Caleb, Landon and Lucas Bradley.

My grandchildren are the highlights of my life.

FORWARD

My son, Gary, brought to my attention the 1903 newspaper article containing The Confession located next to a Joseph Usher article.

My imagination began to wonder what the story could be that went with this confession.

In early American history the 1876 gold rush, in the Dakota's, was a lawless time.

The Gold Digger's Confession is what I imagine could have happened to the characters in my book.

My story takes you back to another place and era. "The Gold Digger's Confession reminds us that we can run out of time.

Chapter One

40 Maple Street

The guttural scream pierced the peaceful stillness of the boarding house. Even the fat raccoon, lumbering just outside through the garden rows, paused by the waist-high corn. All the boarders slept on except for Gabby Snow, the owner, who much like a mother with a house full of needy children, kept an ear out for trouble.

This was the third scream in a month from her boarder, LeBarge, whose room was directly above Gabby's, allowing the deep man's voice to reverberate through the wooden floor boards and into her bones. Gabby was no stranger to boarders in distress. Now in her fiftieth year of life, and having supported herself alone for more than fifteen years, drifters and troubled souls had clumped up her uneven porch steps, hungry for good food and someone kind to listen to their sorrows.

Gabby's two story clapboard house was perched on the outskirts of Pittsburgh, just far enough from the hustle and bustle that there was a sense of serenity when you entered the front yard through the gate she always kept open. Once on her property, visitors found seclusion behind her tall lilac bushes that bloomed so heavy in springtime, a floral scent permeated the neighborhood and inspired men returning home to their wives at the end of a long work day to steal a sprig or two. Gabby never protested. There was also a row of tall and slender pines framing her property, dropping fine balsam needles on the ground, which kept the weeds at bay and provided a home to a host of creatures who added their own charm to those who adored nature. Owls, and chipmunks and noisy woodpeckers were the inhabitants of the screen of pines, and truth be told, Gabby preferred these creatures to most of the folks who crossed her path. This preference she would never admit aloud.

Gabby's business was taking care of people, and she did it well and without complaint. She had seen enough in life to know, that a person who harbors a grudge cannot conceal his or her disdain. In due time, the frown lines, the narrowing of the suspicious eyes, the mouth too reluctant to smile, all betray the one who hates. When life got too much for Gabby, she put on her gardening gloves, pulled her straw hat on top of her thick salt and pepper curls, and poured her energies into the soil and plants that grew with abundance from it. Only when she had the time to be alone in this earthen bed would she mutter under her breath, "God darn it! Give me strength to deal with these fools!" and let her grudges go as she ripped up the invading weeds.

Gabby sat upright in bed, her head coming to rest against the cold wrought iron headboard. The scream coming from LeBarge's room was the cry of a man who had not let go. Even at three in the morning, covered by thick blankets and the haze of fatigue, this much she knew. There was a shuffling across his bedroom floor to his water jug, and then a shuffling back to bed. Only when she heard the creak of her anxious boarder's bed, and could sense he had settled back down, could she close her weary eyes and beckon sleep to return.

Chapter Two

The Day Begins

Gabby was usually the first one up even if the boarding house was full. There was no better time of day for her than the solitude of dawn to clean herself up, then get the breakfast table set and the coffee brewing. She took a pride in her home, as well as her business of providing a home to those without, and something that she knew meant a great deal to most boarders was the smell of biscuits or muffins baking, accented by her freshly brewed coffee. There were not enough hours in the day, however, so to keep her house running smoothly, Gabby had learned enough over the years to employ the help of others to lighten her load. Ann came most mornings to bake the fresh bread for the day. The two women mused over the loaves of rye, wheat and white bread that were consumed long before Gabby had a chance to turn them into her vanilla bread pudding. Her old friend, John, came to help with the vegetable garden when mornings and evenings permitted. The sound of his hoe moving the dirt, and his recognizable whistle were soothing to Gabby. She liked certain things to be the same, things she could rely upon. Gabby was known for her spirited nature that no man risked trying to tame since her husband, James had passed away—long before her hair had begun to silver.

4

If time allowed, Gabby would pour a cup of coffee and sit out on her front porch to watch the world awaken bit by bit. She had memorized the sun's light in various seasons, how it grew from winter to summer and then receded as surely as it had come. On this particular summer morning, the air was cool enough to conjure up autumn, but Gabby knew by midday, the balminess would settle throughout the house, causing doors to stick and her coveted brown sugar to turn into a solid brick of sweetness.

Gabby reclined in her favorite rocker, with a slumped wicker seat, and took her first sip of hot coffee. She closed her brown eyes and breathed in deeply.

"Mornin'." The gruff male voice startled her meditation.

"Oh, good morning. You came downstairs without much racket," she answered.

"That's me—quiet as a church mouse."

Gabby searched LeBarge's lined face for some recognition of his cry in the night but saw no indication. His well-tended beard hid some of his emotions as well as a barely perceptible scar, tracing his strong jawline. She decided, as usual, to refrain. "You sleep well?"

"Bits and spurts. Can't remember when I last had a full night's sleep."

"Let's get some coffee then," she offered, as LeBarge gave her his strong arm to raise her up from the rocker. "Gotta get ready for breakfast anyway...the day begins."

Gabby looked towards the front porch door and saw her Caleb behind the screen, his large eyes widely awake as only a boy can be no sooner than his bare feet hit the floor. "Morning, Caleb. Hungry?"

5

"Yes, Grandma," he answered as surely as she knew he would. "Flapjacks and jam?"

"Flapjacks and jam it is. And for you, Mr. LeBarge?"

"Mr. LeBarge wants the same," Caleb announced, grinning at his favorite boarder. "I'll fight him for 'em."

"No fight from this guy…not today. I'm afraid even your Grandmother's flapjacks won't agree with me this morning. Just coffee will do for now."

Gabby smoothed her cotton apron and gave her boarder a longer look. There was a definite correlation between his disturbed nights and lack of appetite. But she didn't have time to dwell on this for long since the other boarders were making their way out of bed and downstairs for a bit of early morning conversation and a hot breakfast. The table was set for ten, and every wooden seat was sure to be filled by seven am.

"Mr. LeBarge?" Caleb sat down next to his friend. "You said if I got all the wood down cellar you'd tell me the beginning of your gold rush story."

"I did."

"It's all stacked neat the way Grandma asked me. Do you have time today?"

"If your Grandma says it's okay, then you have a deal."

Caleb's face lit up the way LeBarge remembered his used to when he was young. He wondered where that innocence and excitement had gone. Perhaps it was left in the Badlands, in exchange for the shelf of gold he had taken from the Earth—something he would impart to the boy when he told his story.

Chapter Three

The Straight and Narrow

As the boarders drifted downstairs, one by one, all dressed for a day's work—some in paint-splattered coveralls, some in starched and pressed office attire, LeBarge went against the traffic and back upstairs to his bedroom, clutching a fresh cup of coffee that Gabby had just poured from the coffee urn.

He was not feeling particularly chatty, at least not with anyone outside of Gabby or Caleb. Although he would never admit this aloud, for the first time since he was a child, LeBarge felt he was at home. Gabby created an atmosphere of warmth and hospitality at 40 Maple Street. This was reflected throughout her house—in her furnishings which were worn but comfortable, in the soothing music she played most evenings, and certainly in her incredible cooking that permeated the boarder's rooms and brought them together for meals so large not a person left Gabby's, after a stay, with a loose waistband. All these things together, reminded LeBarge of his mother's house, before the fire in his seventh year of life that had reduced their wooden cottage to dirty ash and debris; before his mother had succumbed to consumption in her thirtieth year of life, leaving LeBarge an orphan too old for anyone to consider adopting even in passing.

The sun poured into his bedroom, which was spacious and furnished to his liking. He had a small desk and chair for penning his occasional notes and letters, and a comfortable chair to ease himself into when his bones were complaining. His bed was made up tidily, but if he had left it a rumpled mess, LeBarge would have felt tempted to crawl back beneath the covers and shut his eyes against the morning light. He coughed and felt the ache in his chest, sipped his coffee in an attempt to ease it out, and then settled back in the chair which looked out on Gabby's garden.

Whether or not he dozed, he was not certain, but soon the house was quiet all but for Gabby's call off the front porch.

"Caleb, where have you gotten to? You were supposed to help with the weeding this morning, young man!"

LeBarge could hear some mutterings.

"John needs you in the garden now, Caleb, not when you feel like it."

"Georgie asked me to go to the fishing hole with him. Why can't I go?"

LeBarge grabbed his empty coffee mug and headed downstairs to the porch.

"Here you are," he said to Caleb. "We're supposed to have some time together today—you and me—am I right?"

"Yessir," Caleb answered, staring sheepishly at his scuffed up boots. "I finished the wood pile."

"Well then, Gabby, when could I have your grandson for a bit? We have some important matters that need to be discussed in private."

"After he helps poor John in the garden, he's all yours, but that means no Georgie today. You know I don't approve of that boy, Caleb."

Caleb seemed as though he were about to quarrel with his grandmother, but LeBarge gave him a look. "Well that seems fair enough. Go help out John, he's been having a terrible time with those weeds, and I think I heard him cussing up a storm over the beaver who keeps stealing his corn before it's even had a chance to grow proper. Then we can go fishing for your Grandma, get some brook trout for supper, and discuss those matters we've been putting off."

Caleb stood up straight and nodded, running off towards the garden with determination.

"Thank you so much," Gabby said. "He's become such a handful and I especially worry about some of those boys who come around calling for him…I just know they're up to no good."

"No problem at all. It wasn't so very long ago that I was a young boy getting into mischief. I know a trick or two to keep him on the straight and narrow." LeBarge sat down on the front steps. Gabby noticed the perspiration on his forehead which made him look like a man who'd just returned from his outdoor labors.

"Has your appetite woken yet? Ann's bread is sitting in the kitchen, still warm and waiting for some butter and jam."

"That sounds just about right," he answered.

Chapter Four

Favorite Boarder

After breakfast the boarders scurried out of Gabby's house, most of them heading off for a long day's work. Fred went off to help at the local ice house, Thomas went out looking for whatever work he could find. And LeBarge, who had been under Gabby's roof for nearly four straight months, was the only boarder who didn't have to work. Gabby didn't ask any questions. He was on time with his rent money, and he helped Gabby with chores she didn't have the chance to ask him to do—like repairing the screen in the front porch door which Caleb insisted pushing on each and every day no matter how many times his Grandmother reminded him. Or fixing the wheel barrow that John used while he tended the garden or to help Caleb bring in the wood for the stove. Once Gabby found LeBarge coming out of the cellar, covered in soot and ash almost beyond recognition.

"What on Earth are you up to?" she asked.

"Just gave your stove a cleaning so Caleb has an easier time keeping it stoked," he replied. Gabby shook her head as if she protested his generous gestures, but LeBarge could see the gratitude in her kind dark eyes and for the first time since he could remember, he was finding contentment in a relationship with another person. LeBarge had a crooked half-smile he had forgotten, but these days it seemed to find a resting place where a scowl had been planted for too many years. Gabby noticed his smile and found she needed the sight of it several times a day—just because.

In the evenings, after supper was done and the dishes were washed and dried, Gabby sat in the living room at her upright piano, made from deep walnut and engraved with subtle flowers and vines. This piano had been a gift from her parents when she was a girl. Forty years ago her fingers could barely spread to press the ivory keys but now her hands were strong and confident, and most of the boarders found this reason enough to sit and visit after dinner, changed from their work clothes, propped on Gabby's comfortable sitting chairs and settees as she played everything from Mozart to popular tunes of the day that got feet tapping and heads nodding to the melody.

This was LeBarge's favorite time of day—the sun sinking beyond the back yard of the boarding house, casting muted crimson or lavender light all around them, Gabby's music filling the rooms, his stomach full with her fresh vegetables and tender meat, more often then not followed by her homemade bread or rice pudding and a cup of hot coffee too.

Already, on this particularly warm morning, LeBarge was anticipating the evening hours in his new home. Every so often he imagined the living room being empty except for Gabby and himself, but this was something he knew would never happen. Gabby was the type people sought out. Women loved confiding in her, and more often than not LeBarge would overhear Gabby in the kitchen, preparing a meal, the sizzling of onions being sautéed in her cast iron skillet, or the clinking of her glass jars as she put up more vegetables from her garden—cucumbers made into bread and butter pickles, tomatoes stewed for sauces, strawberries turned into sweet and sticky jam. And behind the kitchen sounds would be the chatter of one of her neighbors or friends sharing her woes or triumphs as Gabby lent her sympathetic ear. When happy news was being shared, LeBarge could hear Gabby's deep laugh—the only sound that rivaled the tunes she played on her piano. If the mood was somber, LeBarge could hear her sympathetic coos and tender whispers of advice. Much to LeBarge's dismay, plenty of men came by too. Their visits were tough to ignore as raucous banter and knee slapping seeped through the floorboards or spilled out onto the front porch where LeBarge was trying to smoke his pipe in peace. Gabby was loved by all, and there was no mistaking why.

LeBarge sat on the front porch and watched Caleb from the corner of his eye. The boy was working half-heartedly in the garden, a row over from John, picking the stones from the soil and pulling the hearty weeds out by their stubborn roots. A gangly young boy entered Gabby Snow's front gate and made a bee line for the back garden.

"Caleb? You coming along today?" he asked with a piece of long grass stuck in the corner of his mouth. LeBarge recognized the boy as George and knew for a fact he had seen him trying to pickpocket unsuspecting people in town just the week before. He understood why Gabby didn't want her grandson keeping company with this troubled kid.

Caleb glanced up from the garden bed and squinted at George in the bright sun. "Nah, I have too many chores today," he responded as LeBarge stood on the porch to keep a watchful eye out.

"This is the last time I'm gonna ask you to come. Tell your Grandmother you can do your chores later. We got things to do. More important things."

LeBarge walked down the wooden steps. "Morning, George," he said.

The boy barely acknowledged the greeting or gave LeBarge a glance. "I said, good morning, George," he repeated.

This time the boy took the piece of grass from his mouth and made eye contact with LeBarge. "How do you even know my name?" he asked.

"Caleb has important plans today, don't you son?" LeBarge said.

Caleb paused. Even John stopped weeding and put his hands behind his tired back.

"Remember, Caleb?" LeBarge reminded him.

"Yes, sir. Sorry, George. I forgot I have stuff to do with LeBarge today."

"Suit your self," George hissed, shoving the grass back in his surly mouth.

LeBarge didn't say a word. He just walked over to Caleb and gave him a pat on the back before heading back to the front porch where Gabby waited quietly with a chilled glass of minted ice tea for her favorite boarder.

Chapter Five

We Found Gold

Caleb finished his morning weeding chores with John. They were a capable team, clearing the rows of vegetables, and securing the tomato vines to stakes with twine— all of Gabby's cherry, plum and beefsteaks kept off the soil to ripen evenly in the summer sun. Now it was time for John to grab some lively conversation with Gabby. He loved her lilting voice and all her curious tales of the neighborhood. He and Gabby had been friends since childhood and in all those years he had never grown weary of her company. John lumbered up to the porch to ease his tired body down into a cushioned rocker.

LeBarge was surprised to see Caleb remain in the garden even after his chores were done. There was no doubt he had an affection for that eleven year old boy, mostly legs, with his mess of brown wavy hair that refused to lay down even on Sunday mornings when his grandmother took to him with a hairbrush and beeswax pomade. "This is a cow's lick like I've never seen," she'd comment each and every week, with a glint in her eyes and a clucking of her tongue.

LeBarge watched Caleb walk the rows of vegetables just growing, the tomato vines coaxed up wooden stakes, newly budding lettuce—pale Boston and lacy Bibb, and the flowers that accompanied the squashes and pumpkins which had yet to mature. Caleb loved the smells of his grandmother's garden—the patches of chives she used in her cooking and dried to put in her boarder's rooms with clusters of blue violet hydrangeas. The mint was his favorite and he often plucked a leaf when she wasn't looking to breathe in its sweet scent before putting it in his mouth. LeBarge felt a tugging as he watched the boy, he felt a need of taking Caleb under his wing and trying to do some sort of good. LeBarge understood not having parents, and although he knew Gabby was the boy's surrogate mother, and a perfect one at that, he was a big believer in boys needing male guidance to find their way in the world. If LeBarge had it his way, he would stick by Gabby's side and see to it that her grandson had every opportunity possible to get the foundation he needed.

"Caleb, you forgetting our plans to go fishing?" LeBarge called from the porch railing. Gabby took a sip of her cold drink and smoothed her apron as if she didn't hear a word.

"I almost forgot to tell you about old Mrs. Needham," she said to John. "Honestly, this is the sweetest thing I've heard all year…"

LeBarge gathered the fishing poles and a tin pail that held their lunch. As much as he could remain all day and listen to Gabby's conversation, he was eager to spend some time with her boy. Times like these, focusing on Caleb, made him feel young again, as if his knees weren't protesting and his hair wasn't thinning.

Can I go now, Grandma?" Caleb asked, squinting in the sunlight through his bangs, which needed a trimming.

"May I please go now?" Gabby reminded him.

"Yes, that's what I meant," he answered.

"You may. Now be a good boy for Mr. LeBarge and bring us home some trout for supper." Gabby watched her grandson and LeBarge disappear through the back path and into the wooded landscape beyond her house. There was a peacefulness in the sight of them, side by side, she had not experienced in a very long time. LeBarge's baritone voice faded as they vanished into the tree line.

"You sorry not to be with your friends?" LeBarge asked.

"Nah, not so much. I want to hear your stories of the Gold Rush."

"All right then. You'll be getting an earful," LeBarge laughed. "When I was just about your age, I knew the one thing I didn't want to be was poor."

"Did you wanna be rich?" Caleb asked.

"I supposed I did. I reckon I'd seen far too many people struggling for food to put in their bellies and clothes to put on their backs. I remember thinking there had to be more to life than struggling."

"Like gold!"

Caleb and LeBarge sat by the brook, where it spilled into the fishing hole. They baited their hooks and cast their lines into the deeper water.

"I'm going to tell you things I've told no one else before you and I will tell no one else after you."

"Why me?" Caleb asked as he stared into the murky water. The boy could just make out the large trout that moved slowly and did not seem eager to take the worms off their hooks.

"Maybe it's because you remind me of myself when I was a boy. What do you know about the Gold Rush in the Black Hills of Dakota?"

"Not much."

"But you've learned about General Custer and the Massacre at the Little Big Horn?"

"Yup."

"Well it was General Custer who discovered gold in those hills and people like me and my friends went out there to make our fortune. California had pretty much run dry and this was a whole new opportunity… but with some big risk attached."

Caleb's eyes searched LeBarge's. "You mean because of the Indians?"

LeBarge nodded. "We took our lives into our own hands many times over but we were the fortunate ones. We found gold." LeBarge reached deep into his front pocket as Caleb watched. The boy believed he was fishing for his pipe and tobacco but instead LeBarge held his fisted hand out for his young friend.

Caleb felt something small and cold drop into his open palm and found a nugget of yellow gold the size a shooter marble. The boy dropped his fishing pole and let out a gasp that made LeBarge's laughter travel all the way to Gabby's front porch.

Chapter Six

Homestake

Iowa felt as far away and shadowy as the last time LeBarge had laid eyes on his mother. There were just over a thousand miles covered between his home and the hills that rose up towards the sky like dark phantoms—they were so dense with trees and brush it didn't seem possible any living creature could traverse them. LeBarge stood for a time and gazed at the foreign landscape. He didn't much believe in premonitions, but as he blinked his eyes at those Black Hills, he had the strangest knowing that his luck was about to change. He tried to stuff that feeling down, as if by reveling in it, even for this small quiet time, he would jinx himself irreparably. More than likely this was no sort of premonition at all. He had traveled all this distance based on the stories that had spilled from strangers' mouths as they sat in the pub, filthy dirty from a full day of work, guzzling beer and shooting back whisky from glasses that were left no longer than a heart beat on the dark wooden bar. For two years LeBarge soaked in prospecting tales and alcohol. In the morning, rising for another day of back-breaking labor, the alcohol had dissipated but the tales had not. They clung to LeBarge and invaded his thoughts during his waking hours, his dreams during his dead slumber.

LeBarge was skeptical about some of the tales, but still he envisioned Lookout Mountain, and a man by the name of Ezra, laden with gold, who scratched the story of his final days into a slab of stone. The night LeBarge was told this story, he sputtered in the face of the stone mason, with grey dust caked beneath his nails and in his matted hair, who recounted it, "You spin some yarn. Don't expect to have me believin' you. A man and his posse are being murdered by savages and he is allowed the time to carve his story before they scalp him?" But then other tales of gold and the Badlands traveled from place to place, carried by weary travelers who didn't have much else to tote but their adventures. Everyone spoke of Custer, but for LeBarge, his interest was peaked when he heard about Deadwood and Whitewood Creeks, which flowed like rich veins through the northern Black Hills. LeBarge understood all too well that all the land hugging those creeks was claimed. But this knowledge didn't stop him, or other men like him, from dreaming. Even just a small parcel of sweet earth could yield enough for a tired soul to retire upon.

LeBarge stretched his limbs and groaned, a habit he had formed in boyhood when the growing pains had caused him to awaken many nights from a deep sleep. He peered out onto the hills with stands of juniper and spruce and ponderosa pine. LeBarge was still a kid at heart, and as he took in the landscape he strained to see some new wildlife he'd heard about— like the oversized bison. He set up camp, gathering kindling for a fire to cook the red squirrel he had killed just an hour before. LeBarge had an appetite. He was hungry and excited, and all of his senses seemed heightened. His luck was surely about to change. As the squirrel roasted over the campfire,

LeBarge took in a deep breath, he filled in his lungs and held the South Dakota air until he felt as if he were desperate to let it out. He did this repeatedly, feeling his breath, feeling his heartbeat, his pulse, the rhythm of his being. He gave thanks for his dinner as he removed it from the spit. And he gave thanks for his life for the first time in many years.

LeBarge had plans. When he was done eating and had cleaned up from his supper, he rolled out his sleep sack and lay his tired body down upon the soil. He envisioned the gold that lay waiting for men who were willing to work. He knew about the loose gold that was mixed in the dirt and the rocks and stones surrounding the stream beds. When his eyes were closed he could see water rushing over gold-flecked basins. This shiny vision was like sort of heaven to a man who had to worry and scramble all his life. Just the year before LeBarge had learned of the Homestake Mine, four men who had followed the placer gold to its source, and they had become infamous nearly overnight. He wondered if he could grub stake some partners and if they could be so lucky.

But first LeBarge had some money to earn, and he was to earn it the hard way. He needed funds for mining tools, funds to grub stake some able men who believed in hard work and shared a similar dream. The next day he planned on securing a job that would yield him fast cash so he could find his fortune, maybe a wife, maybe a family and a place to belong at last.

***

A year after LeBarge had arrived in South Dakota, his skin had browned to a color he barely recognized, partly from the dirt he could never seem to scrub off, and partly from the rays of the sun that beat down upon him as he scraped and saved. When he glimpsed his haggard face in the small shaving mirror, he was taken aback. If he squinted and used his imagination, he could sometimes make out the boy or the young man he had once been, now buried beneath layers of tough skin, beard bristle, and lines that had created expressions on his face that had nothing to do with what he was feeling inside. Fortunately for LeBarge the lines around his mouth were reflective of a man who smiled, never grimaced, so he had the appearance of being hopeful and pleasant. There were many in the newly erected town who stumbled about as if they had not a friend in the world. They cursed and spat and complained, and if you didn't get out of their way fast enough, they cursed and spat and complained right in your face.

LeBarge kept himself out of trouble as much as he could. He avoided too much drink, although drink he did, and he avoided the rough women, although women he did mess with on occasion, and he avoided the nasty poker games, although play cards he did more often than not. Needing good money and needing it fast, he took upon a job that most with a sensible head on their shoulders would not touch with a ten-foot pole. LeBarge drove the stage coach back and forth to Wyoming. Driving a stage coach is no great burden, LeBarge could handle a team of horses better than anyone; it was what he carried that caused him to worry as he journeyed through land that was wild in ways no one could fathom until he ran into a ravaged campsite, where some unfortunate newcomers met their fate by the hands of the Sioux. LeBarge had never seen a murdered woman or small child, and he would never rid his mind of the seared image, try as he might, to drive it out with drink or sleep. There was just no way anything right or good could come from white men coming in droves to a place that had been a sacred home to the Sioux. LeBarge could not make sense of his own hypocrisy. He had no problem understanding the plight of the Natives, how it might feel to have all you have known, taken, decimated, used for purposes that are altogether foreign, and yet their savagery, the images of what they were capable of were inescapable, the stories of their brutality...did all of that serve to make his being one more white man taking what was not his to take? For LeBarge, call it livelihood, call it greed, this took precedence over all else.

So he drove the stage coach, sometimes filled with a haul that exceeded $200,000, with trepidation and concealed shame. He was never alone, and this helped, but companionship, even two or three strong and armed men, did not stop the outlaws from attempting robbery. Somehow that premonition of being lucky had held true, but LeBarge worried that one day his luck would run as dry as his mouth when he hustled the wagon through the remote areas of South Dakota and into Wyoming, snaking on a road that had only been in existence for a mere hiccup, created by the mad rush to pull from the earth what had been concealed since the beginning of the beginning. He felt he had socked away nearly enough to fuel what he had come out here for, and by now, having been immersed in the life of these towns, Deadwood, Central City and Lead, springing up before his eyes as each day passed, more people, more businesses, more taverns, more shysters, more whores, more Chinamen importing more China girls, more Europeans, more mud, more waste, commotion and again, more mud. Sometimes when LeBarge sat outside on a ridge overlooking the town, he thought the people resembled scurrying ants, working tirelessly to build, to provide, to exist. On quiet nights after a few drinks, LeBarge walked up to the crest of the hill where the gold miners who met with unfortunate accidents, or succumbed to disease, were buried. The cemetery was growing in size along with the town, and there was something about it that was desolate and dreary, nothing but dirt and wood, reminders of immortality and death no matter how hard you tried to ignore it. LeBarge would close his eyes and picture the cemeteries back in Iowa, filled with the green of the swaying grass, and the majestic trees that gave the bereaved hope that somehow life does continue.

LeBarge had one more delivery with the stage coach and then he was done. His hands were sweating as he held the smooth leather reins, and he tried to relax his grip, knowing all too well that the horses read his mood. This load was the largest he had delivered and he noticed the two guards passed a bottle back and forth, as if a little bit of fire water could quell their nerves. LeBarge was preparing to take a rest from the reins. He was waiting for their typical spot to stop, a clearing off the road, but then he thought of a hold up he had heard about the week before where the guards and the driver were all killed and the entire load was stolen. He heard his inner voice instructing him to vary their routine. As in need of a stretch as he was, he drove past their usual pull off, looking from one side of the road to the other for something out of the ordinary. The guards noted LeBarge's change in routing and became hyper-vigilant themselves. They put their flask away and placed their hands on their pistols. Over the sound of the wagon wheels and the horses' hooves on the hardened road, it was difficult to hear anything else, but all three men strained to make out sounds that would warrant reaction. LeBarge's eyes were tearing from exhaustion and dust, and sweat rings were forming under his arms and on his back, his cotton shirt sticking to his skin. Inside his head he was swearing. He was spewing every profanity he had heard in the muddy streets this past year, combinations he had not heard any other place. Profanity just seemed to work right now even if the words were silent.

LeBarge noticed one of the guards staring off through the trees up ahead and he followed his gaze. The guard gestured with a flick of his head, an unspoken, "Over there." And then LeBarge could make out a staccato hoof beat that did not belong to their team. Like a phantom, there appeared a Sioux on his painted horse, half clothed, his muscles rippling as his horse's muscles rippled, their two sinewy bodies moving in unison. For some reason there was no acknowledgement they were noticed, just a blind ride through the brush and trees, the road not needed, not wanted, and yet he kept pace with them, like some sort of ghostly escort. One of the guards had his pistol cocked, and the other followed. LeBarge brought his own weapon onto the fold of his lap, knowing if they were attacked, all three of them would have to put up a fight. The profanity died down in LeBarge's head and was replaced with the voice of his mother, singing a lullaby he had not remembered since boyhood. He could hear the sweetness of her song and feel her embrace as she tucked him in and pressed a kiss onto his brow.

"There may be others," one guard said, uttering what LeBarge feared. He had seen what the Sioux could do. Images of the slain Europeans returned, the women and children like limp rag dolls on the ground, their faces blank. LeBarge tried to loosen his grip on the reins but his fingers would not relax and his mother's song slipped away just as mysteriously as it had materialized.

The guards warning soon enough proved to be accurate as two other Sioux joined stride with the first, the trio moving in a tight pack off the road, their horses knowing the terrain as well as their riders, as if they had every inch mapped out in their beings and could travel with blinders on. LeBarge watched the road, but also could not help but peer out of the corner of his eye at the Sioux. The two guards faced outwards on either side, fully alert and at the ready. LeBarge wondered if either of them had ever had to kill another man in his life. He wondered if they were capable. He wondered what he was capable of too.

For the better part of ten miles the three Sioux rode alongside and then they vanished. As if they had some hideaway the white man was incapable of seeing through the trees and growth. The guards spun around, their eyes continuing to strain to catch any danger before it caught them. After a spell, the three men relaxed just a bit and the flask was taken out and passed from one outstretched hand to the next.

Chapter Seven

Cry in the Night

Gabby's sleep was broken Friday night. Her tired body and mind was in need of a solid eight hours of sleep, and she did all her usual preparations to set the stage for some deep shut eye—a half glass of warmed milk in her favorite mug, thirty minutes of reading in dim kerosene light beneath her light quilt stitched by her mother over the course of a long and bleak winter so long ago. Never mind her night time rituals, LeBarge cried out into the silence of the night, and the sound of his voice which reminded her more of boy than man, was enough to snap her from the arms of rest for at least two hours. She lay waiting for another wail, but instead heard only the mournful owl from the woods out back, and the pack of coyotes that traveled through the hillside, older dogs with pups who could only yip as they followed their seasoned pack. LeBarge had stolen into her heart somehow when her back was turned and she was focused on running her household and raising her handful of a grandson. Great strength was needed not to tiptoe into his room and sit by his side or slip beside him and press her body close, just so she could keep those nighttime demons away.

In the strong morning light of summer, Gabby smoothed her hair and splashed cold water on her face, hoping the puffiness under her eyes wouldn't put off her boarders. She knew how to rise above fatigue, grief, and all the worries that could bring even the strongest man down. Her boarders were never greeted in the morning with a glum or reticent Gabby. Laughter was a necessity, Gabby believed, and she made it her mission to bring a few melodic sounds of happiness from her boarders before they made their way out into the chaotic world to earn their wages.

Anne was already in the kitchen, a cloud of flour rising around her from the counter top as she sifted with her arm raised above a loaf of kneaded and shaped dough that would be baked and eaten before its heat had dissipated.

"Morning, Anne. How are the little ones?"

"A handful as always," Anne responded.

"Don't forget how quickly these years pass. Soon you'll be an old grandmother like me wistful for the days when your girls were little and their troubles were little as well."

"So I'm told." Anne opened the oven and slid in her perfect loaf of sourdough.

Gabby reached for her brown pottery crock on the upper most shelf. She needed a stool to reach.

"You don't need to pay me just yet," Anne assured her. "I still have some pies I want to make before those berries go to waste."

Gabby reached her hand into the crock as a look of concern clouded her eyes. "Anne, something's wrong here. I know there was more money than this the other day."

"What's missing?"

"I need to count to be sure, but I am worried." Gabby dumped the contents of the crock on her slender upright desk. She separated the coins from the bills and counted to herself as Anne waited in silence. "Just what I thought. There's five dollars missing."

"That's a lot of money. Are you certain?" Anne wiped her hands on her apron. She knew her friend was not one to misplace anything, let alone her household money.

"Oh, Anne. This is not good."

"When did you last put money in? Are you sure you didn't pay anyone? Think—ice delivery, or the knife sharpener? I thought I heard his bell the other day."

"Yes, but this money was there after I paid them both. Who would have taken it?" Gabby never liked to entertain an uncharitable thought about anyone, especially the people who lived beneath her roof. To allow strangers to sleep and eat and share the same home, you had to be somewhat trusting as well as somewhat astute. There were men and women Gabby had turned down over the years when something didn't feel right. Some people made her uneasy before a word was exchanged. She once watched a man open her front gate and make his way up her front walk with all he owned slung over his shoulder in a bursting sack. He needed a long soak, and so did his clothes, but his lack of cleanliness wasn't the problem. Gabby's favorite cat, Fred, took one look at the potential boarder and streaked out of his path and under the porch of the house. Fred loved everyone. In fact, Gabby sometimes didn't see her Calico for days as he roamed the neighborhood in search of the best grub. Gabby had no trouble shaking her head and telling the traveler, "We are all full up," as she left the porch and closed the door behind her. There was not a single boarder beneath her roof whom she deemed sketchy or would accuse of stealing from her crock.

LeBarge stood in the kitchen doorway, looking more exhausted than Gabby. "Morning, ladies."

Gabby was lost, gazing down at the money spread over the wooden desktop.

"Coffee?" Ann asked.

"Yes, Ma'am. I can help myself…you two are busy." Gabby still said nothing— which puzzled LeBarge. "Gabby, everything okay?"

"No not really. I seem to be missing five dollars from the crock, and I needed that money to pay Anne this morning as well as get some groceries."

"I can help you there, but we need to figure out what happened to your money."

"No no. I can't accept your generous offer but thank you anyway." Gabby sat on the kitchen bench as Caleb appeared having smelled the baking bread.

"Morning, son," LeBarge said. Caleb froze at the sight of the crock on his grandmother's desk and the money spilled out all around it. The boy stared at his feet suddenly quiet. "Excuse us," LeBarge said, taking his coffee cup and guiding Caleb out onto the front porch. "Caleb?" was all he had to say.

"I'm sorry. Remember those kids grandmother doesn't want me around? Well I got into some trouble with them and nothing I could say or do would make them leave me alone except to give them money. I was hoping to replace it somehow before she noticed it was missing by doing chores around the neighborhood."

"What sort of trouble, Caleb?"

"I knew that they were pickpocketing and stealing, and they expected me to join them but I refused. Now they think I believe I'm better than they are and that I'll tell someone, so they say I have to pay them every month or I will regret it for the rest of my life."

"Okay. First things first. You need to tell your grandmother. Otherwise she may accuse one of the innocent boarders. Then you and I are going to make sure that money is repaid. Then I will handle the hooligans."

"Do we have to?" Caleb asked but didn't bother waiting for LeBarge's next words as he held the screen door open for the boy to make his way inside to his grandmother.

Chapter Eight

All Tangled Up

Caleb bounded up the wooden stairs, taking two steps at a time, still wearing his boots despite his grandmother's constant request that he leave them in the mud room just off the kitchen. He paid no mind to the clumps of dirt that marked his trail. "Why don't you go and check on him?" Gabby had just moments ago suggested to her grandson who didn't need much prodding. "You could bring him a cup of coffee…" she was saying but Caleb was already gone.

The boy knocked on LeBarge's door with a light rap of his hand that was sticky with maple syrup. Breakfast had been served, the boarders had eaten and departed for the day, but LeBarge had not even appeared for his first cup of coffee.

"That boy sure is fond of your boarder," John said, having come in from the garden for a snack and some conversation.

"I'm grateful. He needs some guidance from outside of me and you. No offense but you're more like a kind uncle than someone to make him mind his old grandmother."

"I don't know if that's an insult or a compliment," John laughed. "As usual you keep me on my toes, Mrs. Snow."

"Someone needs to."

The two friends grinned at one another just as they had done for forty years, beginning in their school yard days when Gabby could chase John down and force him to say "Uncle."

Caleb got no answer from LeBarge as he tapped once more on his closed door. He hesitated and then knocked louder, pressed his ear against the door, and when he heard no reply, no stirring, he eased the door opened a crack. He could make out the form of his friend still beneath his white sheet, facing towards the wall and breathing like someone sleeping.

"Mr. LeBarge?" Caleb stepped inside the room which was kept orderly, almost as if he hadn't lived there for nearly half a year. In five minutes all his belongings could be gathered and no one would be able to tell that he had been beneath Gabby's roof for even a single night. Caleb didn't like this fact. He wanted LeBarge to be like the other boarders whose rooms he snooped around when they were out and his grand-mother was distracted. Some boarders left piles of books and papers, dog-eared letters or cherished photographs. Clothes hung here and there, a smell permeating the room that was foreign, that spoke of other places far far away, other homes, dusty roads, forgotten or remembered, but lingering all the same.

The boy sat on LeBarge's chair and watched his friend take labored, snoring breaths, and then seeming to stop his inhal-ing and exhaling all at once. Caleb held his own lungs while he waited for LeBarge to draw in his next breath. Relief set in as soon as the boarder's ribcage began to move up and down. The boy replayed a conversation he had heard once between his grandmother and Anne, discussing the sad death of one of their neighborhood friends and how he had let out a death rattle that nearly caused his wife to have a heart attack herself while they lay in bed one late night. Caleb prayed he would never hear such a sound and could not comprehend why death would cause a rattle anyway. It seemed to the boy that death should steal a person with utter silence, coming and going like a prowler dressed in black and barely perceptible.

Gabby stuck her head in LeBarge's room. Her heart ached at the sight of her apprehensive grandson. She wanted to hold him to her and shield him from the hurt of the world. Gabby had no problem taking her own blows, but she had little stomach for seeing her offspring injured. With no mother and father here to protect him day to day, Gabby felt all the more pressure to nurture this boy that reminded her of her daughter when he slept, his serene face at rest on the white pillow case, or when he whistled with such joy it seemed his tune embodied an entire orchestra. There was a pleasure and a pain all tangled up together when she recognized her daughter in Caleb.

LeBarge turned from the wall and stretched. Sleep had darkened beneath his eyes. His lips were chapped, and his hair matted down with sweat and oil. The just awakening man was startled by the boy's presence. "What are you doing here, boy?"

"Bringing you coffee." Caleb slid the mug closer to LeBarge on the bedside table.

"Still hot?"

"Yes, and it's black. " Caleb had tried to drink a sip of black coffee and found the bitter taste off-putting. His grandmother and John had laughed as he made the face only a boy can make when he's tasted something foul.

"Thank you." LeBarge's voice was barely audible, his words like sandpaper on his throat. "I told your grandmother I'd help with some carpentry today on the front porch. Now how am I gonna get this ol' body to do what I need it to do?" Caleb smiled as he heard footsteps fading down the upstairs hallway. He sensed his grandmother had been listening in on them, and he was still at the age where he didn't mind her hovering around. Her presence made him feel protected, and even though he was getting too old to express his need for this nurturing, there was an unspoken understanding between the boy and Gabby.

"She won't mind if you put it off," Caleb said. "Wait until you feel better."

"You could tell me more about the Badlands instead."

"What was our deal? You remember?"

"I repaid a dollar and today I go help Mrs. Randles. I think she needs me to paint her porch railings."

"Make sure you do a good job then. Get half the money back in your grandmother's crock and I'll continue the story."

"Yes, sir. I will." LeBarge took a long sip of his coffee and then closed his eyes. The coffee mug rested on his lap and Caleb took it from his grasp so it wouldn't spill as LeBarge drifted back to sleep. Caleb refilled the water glass on his bedside table in case he awoke thirsty, and walked as quietly as a boy in heavy boots could manage across the wide-planked floorboards, shutting the door on his sick friend.

Chapter Nine

The Sought After Ones

The next few days were sweltering and seemed to pass as slowly as dripping molasses for Caleb. He possessed the child's view of time, despite the fact he was growing like the vegetables in Gabby's garden, and seemingly becoming a young man with the face of a child over night. In the kitchen doorway, Gabby had the measurements of Caleb marked in light pencil every year on his birthday. In paler pencil, faded grey and ghostly, were the markers for Caleb's mother, and he had long since passed her tallest height reached by her fourteenth year. The summer stretched before him like a never-ending journey, and the schoolhouse seemed as distant as another continent. When Caleb was not working in the neighborhood, clearing weeds, or the invasive sumac trees that plagued the residents, if they dared to turn their backs for just a few weeks' time, he was camped outside of LeBarge's room, his back pressed to the plaster wall which even in the heat managed to maintain the coolness of an icebox. Sometimes he read *Treasure Island,* other times he took a pile of his grandmother's silver to polish, and worked tirelessly at removing the sooty tarnish until he could make out his reflection, wide eyes and wild brown hair that took on a whole new appearance in the humidity. By the time LeBarge was well enough to take a bath, shave, dress and ease his way down the steep wooden flight of stairs, Caleb had replaced three of the five dollars in his grandmother's crock. His palms had the callouses of a field hand and no matter how hard he scrubbed them dirt remained under his clipped nails and embedded in the creases of his fingers.

LeBarge found Gabby in the kitchen preparing that night's dinner. Anne had already finished her baking for the day and the kitchen held the cloud of sweet cinnamon rolls and blueberry pie. Sunlight and the oven added to the eighty-degree heat and it was only just 8:30. LeBarge wiped the sweat from his brow with his folded handkerchief. "Morning, Gabby."

"My oh my! You are a welcome sight!" Gabby poured a cup of coffee. "Strong enough to add more whiskers to your face."

"I just shaved. Don't tell me I have a shadow already?" LeBarge could see the amusement on Gabby's face, it always radiated from her eyes and the lines that framed them. "I'm afraid I left a black ring around the tub. Give me a scouring pad and some soap and I will scrub it out before anyone else notices."

"That's not necessary. Caleb will be returning soon and he can manage. Maybe he'll be reminded to take a bath himself so we can go to church tomorrow without turning heads." Gabby noticed LeBarge was wobbly on his legs and used the door frame to steady himself with a tentative hand behind his thin back.

"I think sitting on the porch with this coffee would be a good idea. Do you have time to join me?" he asked.

Gabby nodded, took off her apron and poured herself a cup of coffee. She grabbed two cinnamon rolls and a napkin for her boarder who had lost weight over the past days. "Let's see if we can fatten you up a bit."

A hot breeze passed over the front porch, causing an old rusted cow bell hanging from the rafters to chime softly, like a church bell heard from miles away. Gabby stood by the steps and gazed off into the sloping field that ran down to her garden. Waves of heat rose like an ocean mirage, and reminded her that a swim would be a fine idea this afternoon. She and Caleb would walk the mile through the woods to the tiny lake where she had taught him to swim at the age of two. He took to the doggy paddle with ease and his laughter was louder than his exuberant strokes that splashed the water into his grandmother's face.

LeBarge sipped his coffee and felt his strength return. "Penny for your thoughts," he said.

"Oh just happy memories of Caleb as a baby, learning to swim…" she paused and smoothed back her thick hair. "Children carry such joy. Don't you ever wonder where that joy goes as we get older?"

"I believe life has a way of stealing some of it away. Some people manage to hold on to it though. They are the sought after ones." LeBarge searched Gabby's face to see if she understood his compliment.

"I am trying to raise Caleb to be responsible and conscientious but I don't want to rob him of his spirit. I feel he was already robbed of so much. His parents were both taken his first year of life in an accident."

"You are doing a fine job, Gabby. Your daughter takes comfort in this. She knows and you bring her peace. I will spend more time with your boy and teach him about the things he should know from a man's perspective. He does us both good. Sometimes when I am alone with Caleb the boy in me returns and the decades fall away. He's the best medicine for an old man."

Gabby sat next to LeBarge and rocked as she always did, the slightest motion that creaked wood on wood. When she closed her eyes she could imagine being in a wooden boat adrift on a gentle rolling sea. Only half a dozen times did she go out on the Atlantic with her father as a young excited girl, but she could still conjure up the salty warm air and the feeling of being free from the unmovable earth. "Maybe if you're feeling well enough you might join us for a swim. The heat is too much."

"A swim would do me good."

LeBarge and Gabby rocked and sipped their coffee in silence, enjoying one another's company without the complication of conversation. LeBarge felt if you could just simply be with another person and not have to fill the spaces with words, something deepened, something imperceptible and fine. On this morning, he had this sense with Gabby Snow. For this he was entirely grateful.

Chapter Ten

Stroke for Stroke

Caleb's tousled brown hair appeared over the front hedge. He walked as though he were traipsing through knee high water and his grandmother knew it was the heat's effect. LeBarge finished the last of his sweet cinnamon rolls, and all but licked his fingers, his appetite having awoken along with his body. This made Gabby happy. Secretly she believed with some care and home cooked meals her favorite boarder, whom she now also considered her favorite companion, would get his health back. Today she planned on swimming with Caleb and LeBarge, carving out a slice of undisturbed life, away from the needs of the boarders, and the long list of never ending chores that pulled on her cotton dress like a pesky child. "Get your swimming trunks," she instructed Caleb who collapsed on the porch and lay staring up at the slatted ceiling, a peeling robin's egg blue, having been painted ten years back, when he had been a toddler. One more thing Gabby needed done on her list.

They walked barefoot through the woods to the lake. Pine needles made a soft path and it was too hot for shoes. Caleb led the way, his energy slightly restored with the thought of the cool lake water instead of the sultry air surrounding him. No words were exchanged. No whistling or humming as Caleb and LeBarge were apt to do. There was only the droning of the cicada, which rose in waves as if traveling with the heat. LeBarge loved the sound. The insects' din reminded him of how big and mysterious the universe was, all of the life that existed at once. The older LeBarge got the more he was mystified. This surprised him. He could recall so clearly the certainty he felt at Caleb's age and especially in his early manhood, when the answers seemed to lie in the palm of his calloused hands. At some point, perhaps twenty years back, those answers took off like birds in flight and left him dazed and unsure. In watching Caleb the beauty of that innocent and cocky time replayed itself like a melody known since infancy.

LeBarge took in the green landscape, even the heat had had no effect on the lush fields, bursting with wildflowers, or the thick expanse of trees that made a canopy for the wildlife to escape the summer's sun. This place stood in stark contrast to the barren and sienna-colored dried out sea of the Badlands, where he had chipped away at the ground's crust in search for a glimmer of something sought after by masses and masses of hungry and hopeful folks who had migrated sometimes from across the ocean to grab any good fortune they could. There was nothing about prospecting for gold that LeBarge missed, not even the excitement of the arduous search—the thirst, the downright greed that had permeated him to his very core.

This day, this scorching hot day, when his tired and infirm body had risen out of bed after nearly five days of deep but disturbed slumber, this was the sort of life LeBarge had really been searching for in the Badlands. There had been no knowing then what he now understood. LeBarge could drive himself crazy dwelling on the should' ves and could'ves, so today he decided not to let his head go to that pointless place of reproach. Instead he thought about all things having led him here to Gabby, here to Caleb. Had he chosen any other path, had he not found his fortune prospecting, this would not have been possible. He lay by the lake, on the damp gray sand, watching Gabby and Caleb off in the deep water where their legs propelled them along as if they were meant to be amphibious. Caleb dove down under the dark surface and remained below until LeBarge thought he must be able to breathe the water into his youthful lungs. The boy's head would pop up as he let out his held breath and then hoot with bravado at his ability to defy nature.

Gabby's massive head of hair was soaked through and through, and LeBarge realized this was the first he had seen her doused. She swam close to shore, never standing, her white legs kicking and floating behind her, her eyelashes clumped and black, blinking in the bright light. "Come in, you silly man! Don't tell me you can't swim!"

LeBarge needed no more prompting than a challenge to his manhood. He stood and walked just far enough out to surface dive towards Caleb. The water was bracing and exactly what the day demanded to maintain sanity and comfort. "Why don't we just stay here until the sun goes down," LeBarge suggested. "Caleb you catch us some fish down there, cook it up and serve it to your grandmother and me like a pair of hungry otters." LeBarge floated off on his back, spouting water into the air like a geyser. Gabby swam after him, feeling truly at peace. They traveled from one side of the lake to the other and back, side by side, stroke for stroke, like a couple who had navigated far greater things than a small lake hidden in the woods.

Chapter Eleven

Tiny Little Stitches

While the boarders, Gabby, LeBarge and Caleb slept after the scorching July heat had wilted their bodies and their spirits, a breeze turned into a wind and swept away the oppressively humid air, cooling the darkened landscape and on into the large house. The wooden beams and floorboards creaked in relief, as the boarders' breathing relaxed and the perspiration vanished from their still sticky skin.

The rushing trees outside awakened Gabby with a sound that resembled a full creek running through her bedroom. She sat upright and grabbed for her light summer robe for the first time feeling chilled in weeks. Listening over the sound of the wind, she found herself straining to hear LeBarge's voice. She had come to care for him in a way she had nearly forgotten. Some days Gabby strolled into the town, without much need, simply to observe young people in love, recognize the light in their torching eyes, the giddiness that propelled them along, and knowing all the while, she, too, although decades older, was experiencing the very same undeniable emotions. This happy secret that Gabby carried made her smile at her reflection in the rippled, silvery glass above her chest of drawers. All the while she buttoned her light summer dress, or smoothed her thick hair into some semblance of calm, her mouth turned upwards at the corners, forming the laugh lines LeBarge searched for every day.

Gabby tied her robe and stole across her bedroom and then upstairs to LeBarge's door, hesitating there for three or four minutes while she clutched one slightly trembling hand in the other, feeling those feelings she thought had been buried with her husband. For just a moment she felt a sense of guilt, the guilt of someone moving on with life when her loved one no longer graced the Earth. She apologized to her husband in her head and then made peace with the new love coming to rest in her not as lonely heart. LeBarge was not having a disturbed sleep. Still, something made Gabby take the smooth doorknob in her hand and turn it a fraction at a time until it released its latch and she could ease the heavy door ajar two inches—just enough to see LeBarge peaceful beneath a quilt Gabby had stitched herself nearly twenty years back. This made her glad to see him wrapped in her handiwork. She never would have suspected while making those tiny perfect stitches in white thread, doubled for strength, that one day there would be a man she had yet to meet beneath its colorful patched squares. Reluctantly, Gabby closed his door and eased her way back down the narrow hallway and back downstairs to her room. What she could not have seen in the darkness, was LeBarge who lay blinking his sleep away as she had inched his door open. He could just barely make out the whiteness of her summer robe which hugged the curves he longed to hold.

The next morning LeBarge was up long before anyone else had risen to begin another work day. His back was the only part of him protesting as he fetched his tools that Gabby had allowed him to store in the cellar. He stretched himself, reaching his strong hands until they settled on a beam overhead. All those days in bed had tricked his able body into feeling feeble, and he needed to shake this off for Gabby's sake. Each day a list of things that needed doing sprung up before him. Outside, John worked the garden with the diligence of a devoted family friend, but he had his own land to keep up and his age was not that of a thirty-year old man. LeBarge saw brush that needed clearing, and then burning, the stone wall that twisted around the property needed restacking in spots, as well as sections that had never been completed. He planned on taking sizable rocks from the creek, as well as the ones that had been pulled from the garden—stacked to the side so the rows could be plowed without too much difficulty. Then there were all the house chores that needed doing—things Gabby would never even bother to ask for help with and not because they didn't nag at her. Window frames that stuck, shutters that had come unhinged, loose floorboards, woodwork and walls that needed a fresh coat of paint. LeBarge often walked the house when everyone was gone and made mental notes and checklists that he pulled out as he tried to encourage sleep to come find him. He often drifted off mid-way through the to-do list he had created on his own accord, without Gabby's requests or awareness.

His stretching complete, LeBarge picked up his heavy wooden toolbox, the same one he had cobbled together when he was gathering the funds to try his hand at prospecting. These tools, cold steel and hard wood, were dinged and marred by all the hours of labor he had poured into his goal of heading

West from Iowa to the Badlands. These tools were a part of him, his history, his work ethic and his dreams. How much time it had taken to fill the compartments of the box LeBarge could not even recall. What he did remember was the sweetness of the labor and the near taste of hope in his mouth as he strove to save and accomplish something he deemed worthy. The only thing missing in all these younger man's dreams was the woman to share them with, the woman to take his hand at the end of the journey and look him in the eyes with pride, with a look that told him she knew all along he could make it happen. LeBarge now wished that woman had been Gabby. He took her cellar stairs two at a time, feeling only slightly winded by the top, where Gabby stood waiting for him with a hot cup of coffee and her pleasant expression that never failed to show she was glad to see him.

Chapter Twelve

Stones and Stories

Caleb slept in the first morning the heat wave had broken. Gabby and LeBarge sat on the porch after the boarder's breakfast had been served and the dishes washed.

"I cannot believe the smell of bacon and hash browns didn't waken that boy," Gabby said, placing her coffee cup on the porch railing so she could pull her hair back from her eyes. LeBarge admired her profile, the gentle slope of her nose, and the strong cheekbones that defined her face. With each passing day Gabby Snow's beauty became more palpable, like a new moon turning to full, until one night there was soft light illuminating what used to be darkness. Gabby turned towards her friend and her mouth showed she knew his unspoken thoughts, then she glanced down at her feet, embarrassed like a school girl when it dawns on her that the boy sitting at the next desk is smitten.

"The sleep will do him good. Remember those days when your body was growing so fast, if you stood in front of the mirror you could almost see yourself shooting up?"

Gabby laughed, "No, I do believe that sort of growth is a special thing for males. With girls the growth is all inside their heads and hearts, the wheels never stop turning, and the emotions and ideas …well…if you could see inside, you would run like a Jack rabbit for the nearest cover."

Now LeBarge was laughing too. "It's no wonder one has no idea what to do with the other, at least not until the body, the heart and the head have had a chance to settle down."

"Just about at our age, I believe," Gabby agreed.

"Yes, just about when we're ready to kick the bucket."

Gabby took LeBarge's hand, "Don't you go getting all sullen now. No one on this porch is that old." Caleb stepped out onto the porch in time to see his grandmother holding LeBarge's hand. The sight of her being affectionate with his new friend was a good thing, but still, Gabby brought her hand back and picked up her coffee cup. "Well here you are! I bet you're ready for some breakfast after that long sleep."

"I'm starved."

"You need to eat a healthy meal before we get started on that stone wall," LeBarge instructed. "I need a strong partner today."

"And I need some more stories," Caleb countered.

"You have yourself a deal." LeBarge tussled Caleb's uncombed hair on his way off the porch to gather the wheelbarrow, and some tools to help them stack the stone wall with greater ease.

"Are you sure you're up for this, you two?" Gabby asked.

"The heat's broken and this is perfect weather for back-breaking labor. Right, Caleb?"

"Okay, then let's get this boy fed. Caleb, I expect you to make sure Mr. LeBarge doesn't do anything manly and stupid. We haven't had this stone wall completed for a decade, so it makes no difference if it gets finished now. I got used to the sight of it undone, until it seemed intentional." Gabby and Caleb stepped inside, and LeBarge could hear the sounds of the boy's breakfast being prepared, in the heart of the house he had come to adore on Maple Street.

Caleb didn't take long to eat, despite his grandmother asking him to slow down. She had never seen him so eager to get to work, not in the garden, not on his homework, not even for some silver coins from her neighborhood friends. This eagerness sprouted from her grandson's interest in LeBarge's stories from out west, and Gabby didn't know what intrigued the boy most, the gold, the brushes with danger, or the adventure bug that young males seemed to carry with them sometimes for all the days of their lives. As he pushed in the kitchen chair and excused himself from the table, Gabby poured a thermos of lemonade.

"You two make sure you drink please," she said. She watched Caleb bound down the front steps to LeBarge who was already unloading the stones from the wheelbarrow, and eying them like a man putting together a puzzle. Gabby smoothed her apron, and felt a sense of peace, knowing this was going to be a decent day, and her stone wall was at last going to be finished.

Caleb and LeBarge unloaded the heavy stones from the wheelbarrow, some so unwieldy that they were needed on either side to lift in unison, and then lower them towards the spot where they needed the next one to be wedged.

"Watch your feet now," LeBarge instructed. Both jumped backwards a bit as the stone thudded to the ground. "I'm afraid we're gonna need another load soon." LeBarge took his handkerchief from his back pocket and mopped the sweat from his forehead and temples.

Caleb shielded his eyes from the sun, watching his working buddy's hands tremble as he put the damp cloth away. "Why don't we take a break and have some lemonade?"

LeBarge didn't look convinced that it was break time. "We still have a ways to go and I don't want to disappoint your grandmother. How 'bout we get six more feet done, just about my height in stones, and then we can take that break and I'll tell you more about my gold adventures?" LeBarge sat back on the wall for a moment, feeling the shade of the massive Elm tree that canopied over their heads and gave them relief from the strong summer sun.

""Okay, six more feet, but I don't think you stand more than five foot ten," Caleb grinned as only a boy is able, as if his wit was all he needed to make him happy as a clam.

"The sun's getting to you and causing problems with your young eyes. Trust me…I'm six foot even, and have been since I was seventeen years of age."

Caleb stood next to LeBarge. "How tall do you think I am?"

"Maybe three foot eleven."

"What!"

"Okay, three foot eleven and a half. Looks like you may have had a growth spurt over night," LeBarge's eyes glinted and narrowed.

"Well watch what this three foot eleven boy can do," Caleb bragged, hoisting the last granite-colored stone from the wheelbarrow, which was as big as an overgrown pumpkin in

Gabby's autumn garden.

"Careful now, and remember to bend those knees if you don't want a crippled back."

Caleb dropped the stone and jumped back as it rolled. "Don't you think it's strange that stone walls last for so long? You would think they would fall down. Sometimes I think about the farmers who built the stone walls along the fields, and how long it must have taken, and how long ago they stacked those rocks. Now those farmers are gone but their walls still stand."

"You think a lot for a boy," LeBarge said. "I do give thought to what a person leaves behind. Like your Mama…even though she was taken before her time, she did a great thing in bringing you into this world. Now she lives on through you, and you can live a life that will make her proud, and do many of the things she never had the opportunity to do. And your grandmother, she takes care of all the strangers who come and go and sleep beneath her roof. She has no idea all the good she does, how her home is the instrument of goodness."

"What do you want to leave behind?" Caleb asked.

"When I was young I didn't care what I left behind, only what I could accumulate and get pleasure from. Now…now I feel different. I've seen far too much in my years and have begun to learn what truly matters. If I had had a son like you, Caleb, I would feel I had made some contribution to the world. I have no children, have no wife, have no family left that I know of, and so all I want is to do some sort of good that will last."

"Like this stone wall?"

"Sure. This stone wall is a start. One day, some young boy like you will pass our wall and wonder who the people were who took the time to move these heavy rocks into place so that they stood fixed and solid throughout the seasons and the years."

Chapter Thirteen

Second Badlands Story

The summer heat made the manure and urine in the street unbearable to breathe in and unbearable to stomp through. No one in the muddy town seemed to mind that his shoes and clothes were clumped with earth and excrement. LeBarge was drawn to the center of town when he was not working. As seedy as it was, he could not get his fill of the commotion, the gambling and cursing men who seemed just an inch away from violence when their pockets were emptied, the sultry women who were far to eager to please, their lips parted and their eyes longing, the dog fights in this corner and cock fights in another, desperate animals in too close quarters fighting to their deaths. LeBarge saw the men who had profited and the men who had been broken in their quest for gold, and he was determined he would come away from this squalid place with his pride and his wallet full.

LeBarge sat at the saloon, he poured two shots of whiskey down his parched throat and felt the welcome burn after a tiresome day. Two men came lumbering in and stood at the bar in the fading summer light. The dirt on their skin looked like it belonged, like no tub soak could remove the residue. Their clothes were unsalvageable, needing to be burned not sent to the laundry. One of the men cleared his throat. He ran his beefy hand through his red hair and over the coarse hairs of his beard. LeBarge met his gaze and felt instant sorrow. These men were beaten down by life and whatever they had discovered in the Bad Lands had not improved their lot.

"In need of work?" LeBarge asked, not directing the question to either man in particular.

"We are...name's William Gunton and this is Melalley." LeBarge nodded to Gunton's companion, who stood easily six foot two and had the slight frame of a teenage boy and the sullen expression to match. In the corner stood a prostitute with the face of a girl, large blank eyes and cheeks that had not yet lost their baby fat. She was pressed against the wall by a drunken prospector, who spit and slurred in her face as she tried to turn aside. The drunkard grabbed her chin, forcing her to meet his gaze and then his rough kiss. Melalley made a sudden lunge from the bar, spilling half his drink and stumbling over his own dirty boots.

"Back off you filthy bastard!" he spoke in a voice that was unusually quiet and slow. LeBarge had expected different.

The prostitute stared at Melalley with surprise as the drunk prospector ignored the order altogether and continued to grope the young girl, reaching behind her dress and pulling himself closer. Melalley's hands came down upon his shoulders like two unforgiving vices and relocated the drunkard as if he were nothing but a slight nuisance. The girl rushed away and ran for the staircase from the saloon with a backwards glance of relief to Melalley.

"I'm ready for some cards," Gunton announced, and the three men headed for the back with their drinks, and their hats, and a camaraderie that could only be formed that fast in a dirty town in the Bad Lands, where you'd better have a friend or two to watch your back.

LeBarge had decided by the end of the night that he could stand the company of Melalley and Gunton. They were hardworking, they needed to drink and gamble, they loved women, and they wanted something more in life than this. These were the two men he would grubstake, and he was confident the three of them would find some sort of lucky break beneath this hard earth. For an entire year he had worked his fingers to the bone, saving and planning, and he was at last ready. These two men had nothing, and their desperation made the deal easy to strike. LeBarge would get an equal share of their findings. He thought they would balk at his offer but instead they shook hands and stumbled off into the darkness for some much-needed sleep.

LeBarge spent the better part of each day picking up odds and ends jobs, mostly carpentry and heavy labor. There were always new buildings going up, either due to expansion or fire having laid claim to another dry wooden structure during the course of a raucous night. When his workday was done, LeBarge headed up into the hills to check on the progress of the men. He enjoyed the sight of the sluice boxes being filled with gravel and the rushing water, and the promise of a fortune awaiting the three men if God were willing and luck be on their shoulders. LeBarge had tried to use his good sense. He chose a spot he felt was destined to yield the glittery source that would alter the rest of his days. There was no difference between the gambling men did out in the hills and the gambling in the saloons, except prospecting took labor, some men still used metal pans, and on their own could only sift through a hundred loads during the hours of a backbreaking day. LeBarge felt grateful to have Melalley and Gunton to grubstake. He was by no means one of the wealthy gentlemen who had teams of immigrant workers scouring the cliffs for fortune, but still LeBarge felt a sense of pride and accomplishment. Day after day he hiked into the hillside, out of the bustling town with pens of filthy livestock, and past the shops of the Chinese he had never had even the beginnings of a conversation with, past the stores filled with mining tools, shovels and picks and panning bowls. Once he reached his site, he found a sense of peace. Gunton and Melalley never had much to say. They were tired and in foul moods, ready for supper and booze. But their bleakness wasn't enough to squelch LeBarge's hope. There was too much promise in this part of the world for him to go back east empty handed, and he felt responsible to these two men, as if their very lives depended upon him. So he stood and watched, sometimes he joined in for an hour or two, rolling up his shirt-sleeves and exposing his strong forearms, never afraid of a little more hard work.

After twenty-three days the men found their fortune, and LeBarge felt the weight of the world taken off his shoulders. That night Melalley, Gunton and LeBarge celebrated until dawn, surrounded by women and laughter and a light heartedness that comes with riches. Gunton suggested they leave the godforsaken town with their fortune and make their way back to Illinois. There was no reason to remain and every reason to leave. LeBarge had the sense that their fortune could go as quickly as it had come if they were not level-headed, and he agreed that the West was exactly the place to lose it all. They gathered their belongings, LeBarge took every tool he owned, and bid their farewells to the Badlands.

None of the three men was sorry to be headed east, and as their team and wagon made its way slowly, snaking through the narrow roadways, they counted their blessings but also kept their eyes pealed for any unwanted trouble. They had their fortune to protect, and there were many robbers who lay waiting for lucky prospectors making their way home.

At least the weather was cooperating, as it was early September which brought warm days and cooler nights perfect for sleeping. LeBarge would miss the open sky of the west with its broad canvas of stars. How many nights had he lay on the hard ground, his tired head resting on his folded arms, wondering what the universe had in store for him.

The men were quiet while they traveled, trying to put as many miles between them and the filthy towns of the Bad Lands as they could. Most travelers were headed west, not east, other men attempting to chase their own dreams or flee from some life they had never asked for. LeBarge, Melalley and Gunton smoked and chewed tobacco, they drank and stopped to eat when their stomachs rumbled, but for the most part they held their tongues until the booze flowed more freely and the cards began to fly. Gunton was by far the best at cards and his bravado soared the more he won. The more Gunton won, the smaller Melalley's profits from their prospecting, and the greater his foul mood. LeBarge thought they should stick more to women then cards, but they found reason to hassle over the prostitutes along the way too. Melalley gazed down into the dark water of the Missouri River as they crossed, and LeBarge noticed his companion's eyes were a perfect reflection, impenetrable with an unstoppable current. "Tonight we celebrate at the Silver Bow," LeBarge announced as they entered Sioux City. "Let's grab some lucky ladies after we find something to eat other than squirrel. I'm starved."

"I'm thirsty," Melalley answered.

"Better get some grub in you first," LeBarge suggested but Melalley made his way straight for the bar and Gunton was two steps behind him.

LeBarge had come to notice how the women they encountered had some sort of a sixth sense. They could sniff out the men with cash no matter how down and out they looked or how modest their attire. Since the three men had found their fortune, a shelf of gold worth nearly $50,000.00, women flocked about them, preening and grinning as if they were going to a dance, not some squalid room with a stained mattress. LeBarge tried to keep his drinking down and his wits about him. As soon as he got back to Illinois, he planned on parting ways with his two friends. He wanted a fresh start, and that meant not keeping company with companions who found too many reasons to knock on trouble's door.

LeBarge ate a hearty meal of meatloaf and potatoes, and he treated himself to a large piece of peach cobbler even though he was already stuffed to the gills. He leaned back in his chair and watched the scene unfolding in the Silver Bow, Melalley and Gunton surrounded by empty glasses and equally shallow women. LeBarge wouldn't mind the company of a sweet-smelling woman himself, but he was tired of meaningless encounters and that same sad feeling in the morning when he awoke next to a stranger whose looks never held up in the harsh daylight. Tonight he decided he would go to sleep alone, comforted by his success and his hopeful plans. It felt like a tremendous relief to have plans, as if he'd come in from the cold after being lost for far too long. Not too long ago he had been adrift, a grown man who had lost all his dreams along the way to adulthood, but now he felt he had recaptured his youthful spirit and he was determined not to let it slip away. LeBarge wasn't dreaming about anything too lofty, but a solid roof over his head and a kind-hearted woman he could call his wife. He thought of going to sleep every night in the same house, in the same bed, with his wife in the crook of his arm, her head nestled into his chest. A simple dream.

He watched his companions who seemed interested once again in the same woman, a petite blonde with a turned up nose and a frisky way about her. She worked hard to pay equal time flirting with each man, not sure which one would be the better choice for the night. She seemed more drawn to Melalley, who had a boyish charm when he was in female company, but still, Gunton held her attention with his broad shoulders and deep laugh. Two other women stood sullenly to the side, feeling neglected and sour and giving their blonde friend dirty sideways glances. LeBarge could watch the drama all night. People fascinated him, and he felt Gunton was a mystery, a man with a hidden past, and more than likely a false name. He would not be a bit surprised if Gunton had run off from the military or had been in some sort of trouble with the law. If Melalley knew his friend's story, he never let on, even in a fit of anger over a card game or a woman stolen out from under him.

"You want some company?" one of the neglected women sidled up to LeBarge's table. She stuck her finger in the last bit of peach cobbler and licked the sugary syrup off while she studied his face.

"I'll be heading off…it's been a long day."

"Would you like me to tuck you in?" she laughed. "Sing you a lullaby?"

"That's awfully kind of you to offer, but not tonight."

The woman gave LeBarge a woeful look and slunk back to his friends. The tension was mounting over the blonde, and LeBarge decided he'd rather call it a night then try to mediate between the two drunk men one more time.

"Night," LeBarge said on his way out of the tavern door. His friends barely noticed his departure, as Gunton was leading the blonde to a dark corner while Melalley was left standing in the lurch.

LeBarge took in the night air and thought of sleep. He thought of simpler days ahead, a home, a dog or two, a wife and some kids. He wondered if he had had all those simple riches if he ever would have ventured west to make his fortune or if he would have felt he had everything in the world he needed.

Chapter Fourteen

Make Preparations

LeBarge closed the door of Dr. Johnson's practice and felt the last warm rays of the sun on his face. He checked his shirt buttons, knowing he had left hastily. Sure enough they were misbuttoned. No matter how old he became, there were still opportunities to dress himself wrong, forgetting to tuck in his shirttails or button up his fly. Sometimes LeBarge felt like an overgrown boy, although his spirits carried the weariness of a ninety-year old man.

He replayed the doctor's last words while jostling through the crowded main street, all the workers on their way home for supper, some clean-shaven men in pressed suits, others sooty-faced and hands that needed a good scrubbing. LeBarge liked the feeling of getting lost in a crowd, being anonymous but at the same time part of something bigger than himself. He was reminded of being in the Badlands and the rush of eager treasure seekers who were burning to change their lots in life, willing to risk every penny they'd save for the chance of something better.

"Make preparations," Dr. Johnson had said. "There's nothing more that can be done, I'm afraid." LeBarge gazed out of the doctor's window, through the thick wavy glass that needed a good cleaning, beyond the trees on the front lawn, and beyond to where he knew Gabby's house was sure to be. He shook the doctor's hand and thanked him for his honesty and took his steps back to the place he called home in his own head, never out loud.

Dying had never scared LeBarge. Not since he had matured, leaving his baby face behind, leaving his boyish dreams, leaving his almost imperceptible lisp, and the habit he had of fidgeting to the point of annoying teachers or ministers or any adult who demanded his undivided attention. He had not been afraid of dying when he headed out to the Badlands, traveling through dangerous terrain alone or with his two companions, where he could have been ambushed and left for dead. He had not been afraid of dying when he developed serious illnesses that rung him out like a dirty dish towel and made him wish there were a mother to call out to in the dead of night when fevers worsen and a person feels so alone.

Now LeBarge was afraid to die, and he wondered as he was three blocks from Gabby Snow's house—why now?

When LeBarge reached the boarding house he could smell the pot roast dinner that had been already served, the sourdough bread that had come out of the oven within the hour, and a peach cobbler he had seen Gabby preparing that afternoon at her kitchen table, the sweet fruit she spooned into the dessert reminded him of the setting suns they watched in the late summer evenings. He hadn't thought his appetite would kick in, but sure enough a hunger took hold of him that nearly made LeBarge sprint up Gabby's front steps like an adolescent boy.

"You're running late," she said from her favorite chair. "There's a plate waiting for you unless you've already eaten. Perhaps you had a dinner date?"

"No not at all. Didn't I tell you I had an appointment?"

"You did no such thing. You just vanished, leaving no word, no note, like some wayward boarder who hasn't any importance in my life." Gabby did her best to look put out. She examined her nails and raised her eyebrows, forcing them both to laugh when she finally glanced up at LeBarge who stood frozen in the middle of the porch. "I'm sorry, you are just so easy to tease! I haven't eaten either. For some reason I decided it would be nice if just the two of us ate together tonight. Something different. I made an announcement that I would not be playing the piano in the parlor after dinner but ————— offered to play. He'd better get those hands of his clean first—have you seen how he looks after a day's work? You'd think he was a chimney sweep for goodness sakes."

As if Gabby's comment was overheard, a raucous saloon melody unlike anything she ever played came from inside. LeBarge forgot his troubles and gestured for Gabby to take his hands. He placed one hand around the small of her back and led her in sweeping circles across the front porch. Caleb stuck his head out of the screen door and blinked a few times before laughing at the sight of his grandmother being spun like a school girl, her summer dress billowing out around her. When the song ended, the two dancers sat back on the porch railing and took a deep breath, LeBarge's a little deeper than Gabby's.

"I think I'm ready for some supper," he said winded, and gave Caleb a pat on the back. "Did you eat yet, boy?"

"Oh yes, he ate all right," Gabby responded. "And he's promised to clean the kitchen tonight so I can have a rest."

Caleb rolled his eyes, remembering his promise. "Yes, ma'am."

Gabby linked her arm through LeBarge's and they walked through the side garden to the back yard, another piano melody accompanying them, until they reached a table set for two, framed by her favorite wisteria arbor, so full this season that it created a screen of privacy with its blooming sprays and healthy vines.

"I'll just be a minute," Gabby said. "Don't you go anywhere."

"Let me help."

"No need."

LeBarge watched Gabby duck into the back door towards the kitchen, her thick dark hair slightly undone from their dance. The sight of her was almost distraction enough to silence the echoing words of Dr. Johnson.

Chapter Fifteen

Stolen Hearts

They ate dinner slowly, talking more than they chewed, even though the food was perfect and they each had brought healthy appetites to the table. As the summer sky dimmed, Gabby lit the pillar candles and a gas lantern. Neither of them was in a rush to go inside and retire to their bedrooms. LeBarge watched Gabby's dark eyes reflecting the candle's flickering light, and he took in the lulling intimacy of her voice, along with her stories of boarders who had brought her grief or hilarity through the years.

"Rusty was under my roof for six years and four months, and I do believe if his wife had not discovered his whereabouts, he would have remained indefinitely. Do you know he had only put eleven miles between himself and his pill of a wife, Ida, and yet she had been unable to find him. And make no mistake, that woman surely searched each and every day, save Christmas and Easter. I had no idea the poor man was in hiding. He was the timid sort, and hid his face beneath a cap whenever he ventured out or headed to the wool factory where he worked six days a week. I would watch him walk down the block in the mornings, always looking over his shoulder as if he were afraid of his own darn shadow. When he first arrived he was as thin as a wafer, and I would not be surprised if he had a bleeding ulcer. I cooked him mild food, sent him off to work with a pail filled with a lunch that would quell his indigestion. After a few months, the color returned to his cheeks, and he began to talk to other boarders, even socializing in the parlor at night, and taking out his harmonica and playing soulful melodies that still bring tears to my eyes when I hear them in the darkness of night. Rusty's love was for the birds, and he would gather old crumbs from Anne when she was done with her morning baking to scatter for the poor little winged creatures in the dead of winter. He stood in the back field, casting crumbs into the sky and flocks of birds too foolish to fly south descended around Rusty like he was one of 'em. I think if he could have, he would have sprouted wings and taken flight too."

LeBarge watched Gabby lost in her thoughts. "So what happened to Rusty? Why did he leave?"

"One day this woman came bustling up the front walk with an old black Bible in her hands, and a grimace that could make even the strongest criminal weak in the knees. 'Where the blaze is the scoundrel?' she demanded. Caleb took off for the woods. The few boarders who were home scurried for their rooms. This woman was evil. She spit she was so venomous. 'Excuse me?' I replied, having no idea who she was or who she was asking for. 'I know full well that good for nothing sinner of a man is hiding in your home of ill repute and if you don't bring him to me I will turn every square inch upside down until I find the cur!'"

LeBarge laughed at Gabby's reenactment. "She was looking for poor Rusty I am thinking?"

"You would be thinking correctly. She marched up my front steps, tripping on the undergarments beneath her dress, and even more incensed at how foolish she appeared. Her face was blotchy red. I do believe I heard her panting like a dog in the final stage of rabies. 'Who is it you are looking for?' I asked this cranky woman. 'My husband, Charles Baxter, you fool!' Of course I knew no boarder by that name and told her so, but just as I was finishing my sentence Rusty came up the walk having finished his day of work and ready for dinner. As soon as he spotted my visitor he froze, pulled his cap down over his forehead as if he could disappear beneath his worn cap, and then I knew Rusty had been in hiding all those years. There were no words exchanged that I could make out, just her spewing hate and belting him over the head with her Bible—which lost a page or two from Genesis, but this made no difference to Ida. She gave him no chance to collect his belongings or say his goodbyes. To this day I have a box in the garden shed with the name *Rusty* written on the top in case he returns for his harmonica. I believe he had no occasion to play his melodies anymore."

"That's a tragic story, Gabby."

"I could fill hundreds of pages with my boarder's tales."

"And what would you write of me?" LeBarge winked at her.

"Ah now…that would be the story of a man with many secrets who could steal a woman's heart with a wink of his eye."

"Secrets? What secrets? And woman? What woman?"

"Don't you play coy with me…you know very well your life is one you keep well under wraps. Why else do you cry out in the night and scare me to death?"

"You can't make it to my ripe old age and not have some events that give you pause or come back to haunt you in the dark. But you didn't answer my more important question… what woman's heart's been stolen, Miss Gabby?"

Chapter Sixteen

Caleb's Guardians

Were it not for LeBarge and Gabby Snow lingering in the yard after dinner, neither one finding a need for sleep or solitude, the bullies who had been harassing Caleb for nearly two years would not have been caught sneaking in through the back woods, and into the garden. LeBarge was the one who saw the stone sail over their heads in the darkness, like a small meteor that made its trajectory to Caleb's screened window.

LeBarge put his finger to his lips and let Gabby know she should remain quiet as he turned around slowly to spy on the intruders. He was not at all surprised to discover George and his pack of six, stooped over and skulking about like the trouble they were. Caleb's face appeared at his window. LeBarge and Gabby were hidden from all, in the shadows of the thick wisteria. The scenario could not be more perfect for Caleb's guardians.

"Pssssst, Caleb!" George hissed. "Come out!"

"I can't."

"I said come out. I'm not asking!"

LeBarge used all his strength not to leap up and throttle this troublemaking boy. He clenched his hands and his teeth, and Gabby felt the tension rising from him like smoke coming from the stovetop when she was deep frying bacon. She patted his thigh, knowing he was so distracted he didn't take notice. In a matter of moments, Caleb emerged from the back door.

"We got a job for you," George said. "And this time you ain't wiggling out of it."

"I'm not allowed out this late," Caleb replied.

"Another of your Granny's rules? We don't care what your Granny says. Tonight you do what we say. We need a small fry to break into Wilkin's Store through a back window. None of us fit, but you'll fit just fine then find where he stores his money and pass it out to us. We'll keep an eye out."

"That doesn't sound so smart to me," Caleb responded.

George grabbed the front of Caleb's shirt and twisted it in his fist. "What does a small fry like you know about being smart? No one asked you anyways."

Gabby stared at LeBarge with her eyes wide in disbelief. He took her hands in his and held her firmly, not wanting any adult intervention just yet. LeBarge understood all too well that boys needed to be given the chance to learn how to handle situations like these. He had no intentions of letting it get out of control, or of allowing Caleb to break into the store with these hooligans.

There was silence between the boys until they heard the sound of a punch and Caleb catching his breath. "Now you think it's a smart idea, small fry?" George questioned.

"I don't have my shoes," Caleb said. "I'll need shoes if you want me climbing in through the window."

"Go get 'em then and be quick. We'll be waiting in the woods and if you're not back in four minutes we'll come get you."

Caleb took off for the back door and the boys ran like a pack of wild dogs for the tree line.

"We need to stop him," Gabby whispered to LeBarge. She held her stomach where she imagined her grandson had received his undeserved blow from George.

"Let me handle this. Why don't you go wait on the front porch."

Gabby accepted this suggestion although she had the strong maternal urge to take her grandson in her arms and keep him from harm's way. Her hands clutched her dress, lifting it as she walked, and having the need to hold tight to something…anything. "Those damn brats," she muttered beneath her breath. Caleb was the sole reason Gabby worked as hard as she did day in and day out. Being responsible for this child, being the one he depended upon to raise him, educate him, nourish and nurture him, those needs of Caleb's made her life feel like it mattered. When someone, anyone, even another boy, threatened her grandson, Gabby became incensed in such a way she had never before experienced. She felt the urge to grab George by the earlobe and deliver a swift and severe blow to his backside that would make it hurt to sit down at school for two weeks. She felt the urge to whisper a threat into his dirty ear that would make him awaken in the night fearing for his safety. Instead, for some inexplicable reason, she listened to LeBarge's suggestion and she climbed the porch steps and sat on her rocker without swaying so much as an inch. Every bit of her body was tense and waiting. She wondered what it was about LeBarge that made her trust in him so much that she allowed him to manage her grandson's troubles. Gabby sat on her hands and closed her eyes. The house was quiet inside.

The boarders had gone to bed, some bedrooms were illumi-
nated by lamp light but most were black. On peaceful nights,
knowing that her boarders were sleeping comfortably made
Gabby content, but not now.

Chapter Seventeen

Back towards Home

What Gabby did not know, and this knowledge would not have necessarily quelled her nerves, was that LeBarge had done what older males naturally do for boys coming of age. He had given Caleb countless lessons in how to defend himself. Why the boy had not employed these lessons when George punched him in the stomach LeBarge set to find out. LeBarge was filled with an urgency since his doctor's visit. This urgency had to do with two people—Gabby and Caleb, and he was bound and determined to ensure all was in order before he became more ill or succumbed altogether to his disease. In an odd sense, knowing of his mortality made him feel stronger, as if every moment of the day and night carried the utmost importance.

When Caleb emerged from the back door his face was white and emotionless. The sight of his wide eyes, blinking away the darkness made LeBarge sad. He stepped out from the wisteria and approached the frightened boy. "Caleb?" The boy jumped, his laces not yet tied.

"What are you doing out here?" Caleb questioned, rushing to finish tying.

"I ought to be asking you that very same question."

"Please don't tell my grandmother. There's something I have to do and she'd stop me."

"I saw what happened with George. I taught you how to deal with him, boy, why didn't you stand up for yourself?"

"There were six others. I couldn't possibly take on all of them."

"The rest are followers. All you need to do is put down the one they look up to, and you are strong enough to do so. I heard what George is wanting you to do. All your life you will have folks who will try and bully you into compromising yourself and your values for their gain. If you learn to stand up for yourself now, Caleb, I promise you that you will lead a life far better than mine."

"I see nothing wrong with your life. You even got rich and discovered gold."

"Caleb, you will have to take my word on this. I made mistakes I regret and cannot fix, and have lived years beyond you. Trust me. When you are my age and have a worn out body and a wife and children and grandchildren, you will understand what it is I have told you. For now, just trust me. Let's go. I'll stay far enough back that George will not know I'm around, but you will know I'm there if needed. Take him out and don't do his bidding."

LeBarge put his arm around Caleb's back and guided him out of the yard and towards the woods.

The boy did not look happy but he complied. "You'll be here if I need you?" he asked.

"That's right." LeBarge disappeared into the darker shadows of the tall evergreens. Caleb listened to his faint footsteps become nonexistent, and to the hooting of an owl overhead.

He listened to the sound of his own broken breathing and then somehow found the strength to approach the pack of boys who stood in a circle watching Caleb.

"About time," George said.

Caleb did not respond. He didn't want to expend any energy but for what he stored in his hardened fist. George was not prepared as Caleb took a step forward and threw a blow at his larynx with the determination of a professional boxer. George didn't block or recoil. All he did was gasp in disbelief as Caleb's fist made contact. For a moment he remained standing but then he bent over as if he needed air that could not be found. His bully voice was gone, as he was only able to make some lame whimpers. Caleb was astonished. The other boys were astonished too. None of them made a move towards George, some of them backed away, as if they suddenly had some place to go...like home.

"Gotta go," one of them uttered, and the rest followed as they turned and ran for the barely lit village. Caleb turned around and saw LeBarge's shadow under the distant tree line and he wondered if the boys had seen him too. The boy made his way back towards his older friend, back towards his grandmother, back towards home.

Chapter Eighteen

The Kindness of a Boarder

Caleb and LeBarge climbed the front porch steps side by side, neither saying a word. There was no need for talk. Caleb was overcome with relief and disbelief and LeBarge was overcome with pride as if he had seen this child be born into the harsh world, taking his first gulp of air, and had been by his side ever since. LeBarge felt the pride and connection of a father for a son, and Caleb sensed this connection and basked in it like a box turtle sunning on a rock.

"Where have you two been?" Gabby asked.

Caleb had not seen his grandmother on the porch. He had not yet calmed down from the adrenalin of having stood up for the first time to an older bully. In a strange way Caleb felt he had left his body and had not yet returned to it. His grandmother's voice pulled him back but he could not yet speak.

"We had some matters to attend to," LeBarge answered, giving her a wink of reassurance. "Caleb's pretty worn out though and wants to get himself to bed, don't you, son?"

"Yes, sir. Goodnight grandmother." Caleb bent down for Gabby to give him a kiss on his forehead as she always did before bed. One of these days their ritual would come to an end, but not quite yet. Tonight she lingered a few seconds longer and gave his lean boyish arm an extra squeeze.

"Goodnight," she responded.

Once they heard the boy's feet finish climbing the steep wooden staircase, LeBarge sat down next to Gabby and let out a sigh. She couldn't help but sigh too.

"Well? How long do I have to wait to hear what happened out there?"

LeBarge was enjoying her rapt attention. "What happened out where? What are you talking about?"

"If you want to sleep beneath this roof tonight you'd better hurry up and tell me every rotten detail of my grandson's troubles with that good for nothin' hoodlum."

"Now now, Miss Gabby…is that a threat I am hearing from a lady such as yourself? I must be mistaken."

"Tell me!"

"Everything went exactly as it should. Caleb stood up to George as someone should have done a long time ago, sparing us all much unnecessary trouble. I hid from sight but Caleb knew I was there if needed, and he did as I had taught him, punching George in the throat with a hit that surprised even me and frightening the other hooligans away. Trust me, they won't be bothering with Caleb again."

Gabby reached out for LeBarge's hand. "How can I ever thank you enough?"

"There's no need. Caleb just needed a little guidance, and now he'll be fine."

"All my talk of turning the other cheek did him no good."

"You have taught him valuable lessons, Gabby. What you've taught him will make him a young man with honor

77

and integrity. What he's learned tonight will make him strong and help him to one day protect his wife and children. Now where's that peach cobbler and coffee you were promising me earlier?" LeBarge laughed as he led the way inside to Gabby's kitchen that Caleb had cleaned without fault, leaving only two slices of pie and two mugs for coffee on the counter. "Pie, pie, pie!" LeBarge whispered. He reached for Gabby's perfect desert with a watering mouth.

Upstairs Caleb had gotten between his cotton sheets and stretched out, his long body nearly coming to rest from one end of the bed to the other. On this summer night, with a wealth of stars above and fireflies dancing far far below, he felt this earth was a magical place with great possibilities ahead. All this due to the kindness of a boarder who had slept beneath their roof for a short time and come to care for a boy and his grandmother.

Chapter Nineteen

A Real Education

Gabby had decided she would not discuss the George incident with Caleb unless he broached the subject himself. She knew enough about boys this age to grasp that prying didn't get you anywhere—just a door shutting in your face. How different her daughter had been as a teenage girl, chattering away at the end of every day about this one and that one, or the new outfit she had seen hanging in the window in town that she just had to have, or all the reasons why boys were so infuriating. There was an ease in conversation except when she was peevish, and Gabby felt natural as a mother of a girl. Caleb had been a real education for Gabby Snow. Even though he was a polite child, she could tell when he felt like rolling his eyes or sighing when she said something deemed foolish. Usually he just bit his tongue and gave his grandmother a stare that said it all.

The morning after the incident, Gabby sat in the kitchen, keeping Anne company, lending a hand rolling out pie crust. She was already on her second cup of coffee but LeBarge had not been enticed by the aroma to come downstairs for a cup. Gabby couldn't help but check the doorway each time she

heard heavy footsteps, but she only found her boarders looking for breakfast before beginning their long days.

"You sure are distracted," Anne commented, knowing full
well whom Gabby was searching for.

"Not really." Gabby dismissed Anne's intuition by focusing
on her rolling pin, pressing it into the pale dough until the
crust seemed to be ironed flat.

Caleb bounded down the steps and appeared in the door.
"Morning, Grandma, morning, Anne," he sang out as if he
didn't have a care in the world.

"Well, good morning, young man," Anne replied. "Don't
you look as though you grew a good few inches over night!"

Caleb laughed and Gabby noticed her grandson did seem
to be standing taller. She had no doubt he was freed by the
events of the night, and having the courage to put George
in his place as well as not taking part in the robbery. Her
impulse was to wrap her arms around his slim frame and
kiss his forehead, but this would be far too demonstrative so
Gabby stayed put. This need to be reserved did not suit her
one bit.

"You hungry yet?" she asked. "We've got biscuits coming
out of the oven, and a whole batch of bacon. I think scrambled eggs are in order…don't you?"

Caleb nodded and pulled out a chair. "You need me to peel
potatoes or chop onions for dinner?" There was a maturity
just beginning to skim coat his voice, and Gabby tried to remember how he had sounded in the years gone by. Change
was an odd thing. It came upon you, whether you liked it or
not, and then settled all around you until you could barely
remember what had been before.

"That would be wonderful," Gabby responded. "Both are needed for some potato croquettes.

Caleb gathered the peeler, a sharp cutting knife and sat himself down next to Anne. "I think I am growing. Every night around three o'clock I wake up feeling like I need another dinner. I can't stop thinking about what's in the kitchen to eat, so I go back to sleep counting Anne's loaves of bread, muffins, cookies, pies…whatever comes to mind."

Anne laughed. "And does this work?"

"Not really. The pit in my stomach just gets bigger and gnaws away at me all the more."

"A glass of milk is always helpful," Gabby suggested.

"Not for my kind of hunger!"

Gabby scrambled up an enormous batch of eggs, got the bacon and biscuits on serving platters and carried it all out to the dining room where there were a half dozen waiting boarders with gratitude all over their faces. Even though they were all adults, having Gabby bring her home cooked meals to the table twice a day reminded them of being mothered, and no matter how old a person gets, a little nurturing still goes a long way. But even with breakfast wafting throughout the house, LeBarge did not come down for a bite to eat.

"Caleb when you finish up with the potatoes and onions could you please check on LeBarge for me?"

"I can check now if you want."

"No…let him sleep. Something tells me he got tuckered out last night. Maybe he was up counting muffins too."

Caleb peeled the golden potatoes faster than his grandmother had ever seen. He scooped out the eyes and put all the peels in the bin to be spread as compost for his grandmother's garden. He diced the onions, wiping the tears from his eyes every so often, and reminding Gabby that it had been quite some time since she had seen him crying for real. Anne finished assembling her cherry pies, and gave Caleb a pat on his back. "Nice to have you keeping a couple of old ladies company in the kitchen."

"I'm going up to check on LeBarge now," he answered. Gabby heard her grandson taking two steps at a time and then she heard a gentle rapping on LeBarge's door. "Morning?" Caleb called out as if he were not certain. She could hear no conversation over the chatter of the boarders, but she assumed her grandson was talking LeBarge into coming down for breakfast.

Chapter Twenty

There is Nothing to Be Done

When Caleb received no response from LeBarge, he opened his closed door enough to make out his sleeping friend who lay facing the wall. The room was too warm, with the summer sun already beating in, and for some strange reason the window was closed tight, which was not the way any boarder in Gabby's house preferred sleeping. LeBarge lay under layers of blankets, the quilt stitched by his grandmother on the outside but tucked in beneath his chin. Caleb listened to his fitful breaths which sounded almost like an old dog on a too warm day—rapid and nearly pants instead of the peaceful sleeping breaths of a healthy man. The boy didn't say anything else. He just took a seat on the bedroom floor and waited for his friend to stir. As LeBarge slept Caleb remembered the stories of the Badlands he had told him, the adventures that had shaped his friend into the person the boy adored and admired, and even the troubles that caused LeBarge to do things he was ashamed of to this day. Caleb accepted this friend in his entirety and with no judgment and hoped one day someone would love him enough to do the same.

For a week and two days, LeBarge remained in his room, only emerging to use the bathroom and press a cold washcloth to his face. He resented the reflection he caught in the mirror over the sink. His color was wrong—grey and dull, and the whites of his eyes were anything but clear. He smoothed his ruffled hair back into place, knowing Gabby would be coming to check up on him with a tray full of breakfast and a hot mug of her dark roasted coffee. Even the thought of coffee didn't do much for his spirits. There was one thing on LeBarge's mind and he was determined on this day to address it. With wobbly legs he made his way back to bed, grateful to climb beneath the cool sheets and rest his weary head on the pillow.

"Morning, you lazy old fool," Gabby said as she opened the door with a bump of her curvy hip. There was a hot blueberry muffin with a pat of melting butter, and the smell was perfect but could not rouse his appetite.

"Is that any way to greet your favorite boarder?"

"Ah now, you know I'm just trying to shame you from that bed of yours. No harm meant."

"I do have energy to do something that I've been meaning to get to…you think you could give me some assistance some time today?"

"Surely. What is it?" Gabby pulled a chair next to LeBarge's bedside and spread a white cloth napkin over his lap.

"Just coffee I'm afraid."

"Still no appetite?"

"No, I'm afraid not. I need to get something important down on paper and then I would like it delivered to the Post Office General in the event that something happens to me."

"Like what kind of something?" Gabby raised her eyebrows in a challenge.

"Gabby, I'm sorry but I don't want certain things to go unsaid or to pretend that I've got much longer here with you. A man knows when his time is up, and mine is done."

"I can't sit here and listen to you talk this way. We have plans, you and me…"

"Yes we do and it breaks my heart I can't carry them out. You know if I were not ill, we would be planning a wedding, and I would look after you for all the years gifted me. I love you, Gabby Snow, and I love that grandson of yours. You two have given me quite a gift. Don't you ever forget that."

"It's you who's given the gift to Caleb and me. Is there really no hope? I don't think I can bear to hear your answer… but tell me the truth."

"The doctor had confirmed what I already knew. There is nothing to be done." LeBarge took Gabby's trembling hand in his own. Their hands trembled together. They were two frightened and saddened grownups who felt like mere children, but at least they could cling to one another.

Chapter Twenty-one

Letter Writing

LeBarge sipped his coffee without his usual morning gusto. Gabby knew he didn't need his early day fuel since he was just lazing about in bed. Beads of sweat appeared on his brow and he wiped them away with his napkin. For an hour and a half he labored over the clean white paper she had given him. She sat watching as he filled the pages with surprisingly graceful writing. If she had to guess, Gabby would have imagined an illegible hand, more of a printed scrawl that sat heavy on the page. His careful penmanship endeared him to her all the more. She sat with her eyes closed and dreamed about years of love letters written from LeBarge, a thick stack tied with twine and kept stored away in her bedside table, read by her time and time again until the pages were compromised from being folded and unfolded. Gabby's dream dissolved upon opening her eyes as she could determine from the expression on his face, which did not simply reflect his ill health, how much he was suffering. She made a concerted effort not to let any unwanted emotion show upon her face. His written words were a reflection of pent up thoughts and memories, now committed to the page for anyone who cared to read them. She had no idea who this letter was meant for and she stopped herself from questioning him just yet.

Her focus was on LeBarge and helping him with this pressing chore. As he wrote, he sometimes paused to speak, his voice trembling. The strength in his breath and vocal chords was weakened. Gabby wished she could conjure up the sound of his healthy voice, but she could not. Occasionally her eyes turned watery. Then she was quick to stand up, stretch, and walk herself over to the windows to pretend she was checking on this thing or that.

"Am I keeping you?" LeBarge asked.

"Goodness no…just making sure that all is how it should be. No deliveries are coming, no mail, and no trouble seems to be making its way up the front path! So let's continue on here." She returned to her seat. "Do you need anything? You do want me to stay, don't you?"

"Funny, I just had an image of you as a school girl, working away in the classroom. If we had sat near one another, you would have been quite the distraction."

Gabby enjoyed the thought. "I was a Tomboy. If you had messed with me there would have been no telling what the consequences would have been!"

LeBarge lay back on his pillows and sighed as if he had just returned from a mountain climb or a hard day's work. "Okay then. Let's finish this up." He took in a slow and shallow breath and picked up where he had left off. Neither of them knew that resting outside the door was Caleb, straining to hear every word spoken and more curious than a young cat about what his friend was committing to the page. He hoped he would be asked to mail the letter so he could peek inside the envelope and read his sick friend's words. Even this young boy could sense that LeBarge would not be living out the rest of his years to old age.

Chapter Twenty-two

Absence

Without LeBarge to help out around the boarding house, nothing was running as smoothly and Gabby noticed. She was annoyed at this neediness on her part. She had always functioned just fine on her own, and Caleb was turning into a dependable young man. Somehow in the months that LeBarge had lived beneath her roof, bit by bit, she had become accustomed to his helpfulness and his quiet ways of getting chores done without her even being aware. And Gabby wasn't the only one who had come to rely on LeBarge. He had made a difference in the kitchen, helping Anne with the firewood needed for the stove, the heavy blocks of ice to keep the food from spoiling, and the unwieldy sacks of flour that she seemed to make vanish overnight with her baking for all the hungry boarders. In the garden, he had taken over hours of weeding, gathering rocks for stone walls, tying up heavy vines of Gabby's tomatoes, and her sunflowers which were the size of dinner plates and bent over from their sheer weight. If John had been the jealous sort, he may have minded, but truth be told, he wasn't a young man anymore and his back protested after too many hours stooped over and laboring in the soil. Just a week of LeBarge being bedridden and the whole house felt his absence. Even the boarders missed his bellowing laugh at the table, his harmless teasing and easy conversation. Caleb was taking it the hardest.

The boy wandered around the house like he had after the loss of his parents so many years ago. He didn't express himself with words much, but his body language and downcast eyes spoke volumes. Gabby noticed how he avoided her, keeping to himself as much as possible. He often grabbed a book from the library shelves, usually one his mother or father had adored when they were young, and he sat in the dim hallway outside LeBarge's room, sometimes inside, waiting for him to stir, needing a drink or help walking to the bathroom.

"You're a great help," Gabby had told him early one morning. "I have so much to see to around here, and having you keep an eye out is a world of comfort."

Caleb nodded and returned upstairs to his post. He read **Little Lord Fauntleroy** from beginning to end in one week's time. Caleb closed the book when he was done and fantasized about he and his grandmother having an easier life, one in which she would not have to work tirelessly each day from sunrise to sunset. Through the imagination of a child, he pictured one day soon being able to be the man around the house who could provide for his grandmother and take the burden from her of putting food on the table and scraping together the coins to pay the household expenses. Even though LeBarge never would have replaced his father, nor his grandfather, Caleb had fancied him a surrogate of sorts, and a male companion for his grandmother to rid her of her loneliness and solitary ways. Caleb could recall no other grownup who had been so accessible. The two of them could speak with ease, and LeBarge gave him guidance without being oppressive or domineering. Any advice came from his sincere care for the boy with no agenda attached. If Caleb ever had children of his own, he wanted to be a combination of LeBarge and his grandmother rolled into one. In this way, two people he loved would be passed onto the next generation.

Chapter Twenty-three

Blood on My Hands

The branches of two oak trees, still young in years, swayed overhead, the leaves a rustling canopy that allowed the glimmer of stars to shine through here and there. The air was different in Iowa and I pulled a big breath into my lungs, trying to dispel the liquor that had invaded me through and through. The air felt cleansing, and I thought maybe, just maybe, this was to be a new chapter. There would be no more financial struggles, no more back-breaking labor 'cept for what I choose, no more wandering from place to place without a spot I could think of as home. Maybe there would be a missus, maybe there'd be a child or two, a solid roof over our heads and a garden to tend. I let my mind linger on these imaginings as Melalley and Gunton drank themselves into oblivion.

The night was quiet, only one or two road travelers had passed us by, barely slowing down their horses to give a tip of their hats or a nod of their weary heads. There were no lights from nearby houses, gravestones were our nearest neighbors, but fatigue had taken me over and I was in no mood for pub nor hussy, in no mood for the commotion that rides along with drink and women. But my companions would not let go of the card playing nor the whiskey. They passed me the brown jug and waited for me to swig. The cards were dealt as we stoked our fire.

Melalley had the mean glint in his eyes which were already at half-mast. He peered at me from over the fire with a clenched jaw. All the joy he had back in the Badlands, happiness for our good fortune, had been left somewhere along our dusty route to Iowa. Some men just can't help but be miserable. My eyes did not lock long onto Melalley's. Instead I picked up my hand and tried to hush that voice inside of me—the one I ignore when I should pay a mind. The voice said, "Get some shut eye and leave the card playing to these two fools." You learn a few things on this earth by the time you reach manhood, and I had learned to steer clear of angry bastards who want to play cards. Melalley never shook his bad mood all day and his poor horse took the brunt of it. Gunton was not swayed by our companion's darkness, and his mood was elated as he won hand after hand, his posture straightened, his chest puffed out, and his whooping and hollering got louder—all this just put more of the darkness into Melalley's eyes and made him reach more for the bottle. The whiskey poured down his chin. He wiped it with the back of his grimy hand and cursed. When he was done spewing curses he threw his money belt down on the ground as if it were no good to him anymore. He bet it all, $15, 000.00, swearing he would win the next hand. Gunton grinned. If any grin could say it all, this one did. Melalley was too drunk to see the writing on the wall. He threw down four Kings and Gunton threw down his straight with a strong flick of his wrist and a laugh to match.

What followed was more cursing out of Melalley's mouth, a stream of pure venom that he unleashed with accusations of Gunton being a liar and a cheat. Their profanity and their ire rose above the fire, up into the oak trees and into the dark night sky. Time stood still until it didn't, until it sped forward and blurred as it does when discord arrives. A glinting knife in Gunton's hand, a quick lunge into Melalley's arm, screams and grunts and more curses that were harsh enough to raise the nearby dead. I froze, the gash in Melalley's arm was alarming even in the dim night, but it did not stop him from reaching for a wooden stake and striking it against Gunton's head with a force that would have a clear end. Gunton fell to the ground with a thud and lay still, a blank expression gazing up to the stars, not blinking or closing. I moved down and felt behind his ear, the skull no longer in tact, the blood flowing freely like the rivers we had mined.

There is no sound like a dying man gasping for his last breaths. I cradled Gunton's broken skull in my open hands as he opened his mouth and tried to deny death's approach. There was a fear in his breath, as if he knew it could not fill his lungs, nor keep him tethered to this earth. He gasped and then he was gone, and one time more than I would like to have seen, his body became an empty vessel, no longer Gunton, no single thing reflective of the man I had known. I placed his head down and knelt with bloodied hands as if I had done the killing myself.

Melalley and I sobered up at the sight of our dead companion. We spoke not a word but somehow moved as one, dragging him from the firelight and into the darkness, the only sound some distant coyotes off in the nearby woods. I slit off

Gunton's shirt and pants, searching his pockets for any evidence of who he might be, and then tossed his clothes into the fire. The smoke rose up and I stood immobilized for a bit wishing I could rise up too and leave this scene behind me. Out of the smoke I saw Gunton's head, as if he were standing among us once again. The smoke shifted and there stood Melalley, holding the dead man's severed head in his hands by his bloodied red hair. The head swung, the eyeballs protruding and unblinking, as if he were alive and disbelieving what had transpired. His mouth in a cruel sneer as if he were ready to curse at Melalley one more time and demand his winnings. With a careless toss, Melalley threw the head onto the fire and then watched as the hair was singed off, the flesh melting into the scorching heat. The air was no longer pure. An unbelievable stench arose. We took Gunton by the feet and dragged him into the woods, his naked body a stark sight in the darkness. Melalley took a shovel and dug with all the fury and vigor he had shown while prospecting. He broke out into a drenching sweat but did not say a word. Once the grave was deep enough, we dropped our companion and covered him with the dirt, packing it down with our hands and feet, then covering the hole with rocks and leaves and twigs until Gunton's grave was not discernible. Only a bloodhound could find him now.

The stench around the fire pit was worse and I feared discovery of Gunton's head. I lifted it from the fire, sickened by the cooked flesh and unrecognizable features. Instead of returning to the gravesite, I dug a hole in the roadway, directly in the wagon rut, so any traces would be tampered down and lost with the passing of horse and buggy and wagons. With

Gunton dead and buried, the last thing to do was put out the campfire, take its ashes and scatter them over the murder trail, masking the blood and signs of this tragic event. Melalley hitched up our team and we set out into the night, not speaking, and not believing.

The blood was washed from my hands but it was still there. Dawn arrived as Melalley and I were twenty miles away from Gunton's gravesite. Still not a word or look exchanged between us.

Chapter Twenty-four

Unspoken Goodbyes

Gabby Snow had loved and lost many times over. She knew all too well that way grief had its way of creeping inside her and building a home despite her eviction notices and her resistance. As she helped Anne in the kitchen on a quiet Sunday morning, the pale sunlight cast no more than a grey hue through the windows. Gabby worked the dough Anne needed for the boarders' breakfast bread, her famous honey wheat that would be consumed by ten am. As she kneaded, Gabby remembered how there had been no greater pain than burying her daughter, and watching Caleb flounder without his mother's love and affection. Even the unbearable ache of her husband's death did not carry the same cruelty of losing a child. And yet, despite the strength she had learned she carried deep within, with the loss of daughter and husband, this middle-aged woman did not have the certainty that she could abide the pain of saying goodbye to LeBarge. Foolishly, she had come to see her life opening before her once again, like a twenty-year old woman with years of romantic love ahead of her. All this due to the scruffy LeBarge, with his strong and capable hands, and his big and open heart. Even worse, she had come to see LeBarge being a reliable male presence for

Caleb, a father and a grandfather rolled into one. How she had come to fancy this for her grandson. How she had imagined LeBarge would make a difference in Caleb's growing up. Just the one incident with the hooligans was enough to show Gabby the difference it made to have LeBarge beneath their roof. She knew how differently that night could have gone, or how Caleb could have found himself in a world of trouble without so much of a second glance back. Gabby put the bread in the oven and sat down at the table while Anne finished her second batch of blueberry muffins.

"I know your thoughts are heavy," Anne said, pushing a few strands of loose hair back with her arm.

"They are."

"You think the end is near?"

Gabby could not manage to answer with a spoken word. She simply nodded and stared into the pale grey light.

"I will stay with you then. Be an extra pair of hands so you are free to tend to LeBarge. My sister will take care of the children for me. They love when she looks after them since she's got no rules and she spoils them rotten. I know John is prepared to lend a hand as well."

"Thank you," Gabby responded. Anne's kindness nearly made her weep but she was able to suppress the emotion for now.

Caleb shuffled into the kitchen and pulled up a chair next to his grandmother just like he did when he was a younger child. His eyes were still drowsy from sleep and he hadn't bothered to comb his hair. Anne said good morning to the boy but no other words were exchanged as if they had a silent understanding to be quiet, surrounded only by the familiar sounds and smells of the breakfast kitchen, something that brought them all comfort. Caleb moved his chair a little closer to his grandmother's without getting up. When Anne's back was turned, he rested his head on Gabby's shoulder for just a moment, and she smoothed his mussed-up hair into place.

The sad news spread quietly through the boarding house. The table was full but no one spoke except to ask for the butter or coffee to be passed. Those who were especially fond of LeBarge stuck their heads in his doorway to say their unspoken goodbyes.

Chapter Twenty-five

Say My Name

Something about the day carried the knowing and the weight of the knowing that LeBarge would not be with them by nightfall. Gabby Snow felt the weight as soon as her eyelids lifted and allowed in the new light of dawn. Her hands were drawn to her chest as if she could take the weight from her, a heaviness in her heart, that radiated throughout her chest and into her throat. She doubted she had the ability to utter a single word, and yet when Caleb arrived at her bedroom door, tentative and half asleep, she mustered up a "Morning," all the while feeling the hypocrisy of the word. Morning is something you embrace and there was nothing about this day Gabby felt like holding near or dear.

Caleb rested on the edge of his grandmother's bed. He hadn't come into her bed for a long time now, not for a bedtime story or trying to slough off the aftermath of a gripping nightmare. He said not a word. His breathing was shallow as if he were sleeping still, and his hair every bit the mess that it always was. Gabby rested her hand on top of her grandson's and they remained silent as the birds' volume intensified along with the sunlight. Until the sounds of the horses and wagons and the voices of the locals heading off to their

workdays, the calls of children on those last free days of summer, anticipating the chains of the schoolhouse that were just
around the corner.

"Think I'll skip breakfast," Caleb spoke at last. "Just gonna
keep him company."

"I can bring you up something."

"No thank you. I don't feel hungry." Caleb padded in his
bare feet out of the room and towards LeBarge's door.

Gabby carried out all her usual chores, she and Anne and
John made sure all the boarders were tended to, the food for
the day was prepared, the pot roast all ready to be put in the
oven with potatoes and carrots and onions from the garden,
picked fresh by John. The house was filled with the baked aroma of Anne's apple cobbler, so much so that even folks passing by out on the sidewalk paused and took in a deep breath
or two. But the house was hushed. They had played no piano
in the parlor for a few nights now, and the boarders kept their
voices dimmed like they were in a church or a library. Gabby
wondered if LeBarge resented the quiet, and thought perhaps
they should be carrying on business as usual, letting him be
lulled by the melodies of the house. For this reason she felt a
heap of relief when she stood outside his door and caught the
sound of Caleb and LeBarge conversing, two soft but consist-
ent voices that found a comfort in one another. She strained
to hear what they spoke about but she could not and nor did
she feel she should be eavesdropping no matter her curious
spirit that had remained from girlhood. For three hours Caleb
remained closed behind his friend's door, still in his pajamas,
still with his hair this way and that, still unfed. His grandmother recognized that Caleb had awoken with the same

knowing, the same weight of the knowing, and nothing else seemed to matter to the boy but his last hours with his friend.

Gabby and Anne had lunch waiting for the boy when he at last came clumping down the wooden stairs, dressed, washed, and hair uncombed. John made sure Caleb took in some nourishment while his grandmother and Anne checked on LeBarge. Anne brought a basin of heated water from the stove with herbs from the garden to help soothe his tired breathing and his even more tired spirit.

"Thank you, Anne. Could you please leave us?" LeBarge's voice was so raspy it was difficult to hear.

"Just give a holler if you need me," she instructed Gabby. Anne closed the door on her way out, and Gabby felt the oppressiveness of the air, with the windows shut and the presence of something strong in the room. She understood all too well. She longed to open the windows wide, draw back the curtains, fling open the door and get this man out of bed and into the tub. She longed to fill his belly with some hot soup and a few rolls, and take him on a walk down the path, through the dense woods for a swim in the lake. Instead, Gabby lay a warm compress on his forehead and watched him close his eyes.

"Will you send the boy off with John until tomorrow? I'd rather he remember this last morning we shared, and nothing more."

"Of course. I'm sure John has some work he needs help with at home. Caleb loves it there. Anything else?"

"Say my name," he replied and gave Gabby's hand a squeeze. His hand still looked strong, capable. She could not stop herself from staring and longing for what could not be.

"LeBarge."

"No. I need to hear you say my name as if I were your husband."

Gabby hesitated, and then realized she had never used his first name, nor had any of the boarders. She knew his first name. Alone she sometimes let herself speak it aloud. She leaned down until her lips were close to his ear. "Jerome," and then she pressed her lips to his temple. "Jerome."

Chapter Twenty-six

Jerome

The rain was hard and steady, driven sideways by the wind. Gabby was content to stay indoors, tidying the house, nesting as she prepared for the colder months ahead. The shortening days, the quieting of the birds' song in the morning, not one bit of it did she mind. She would not admit this to anyone in particular, but in a way Gabby believed that nature was grieving right alongside her.

Today she scrubbed down LeBarge's room. First the walls with warm soapy water, then the floor, down on her hands and knees with a brush. The wind and rain beat against the windows. Gabby paused from time to time and simply stared at the neatly made bed, its corners tucked tight, the comforter so smooth it looked like the icing on Anne's famous icebox cake. If she tried hard enough, a clear image of LeBarge appeared. Healthy LeBarge, gazing at her from across the room, wanting to know what was for dinner. Jerome, she corrected herself. She must say his name fifty times a day, before her eyelids had opened, while weeding in the garden, working side by side with Anne in the kitchen, the two of them humming with their hands buried in flour-dusted dough, brushing her curls out before bed, turning down her bed and climbing between the sheets—Jerome.

Gabby closed the door on her favorite boarder's room just as the rain was lessening, small specks of sunlight filtering through here and there. In an hour, there would be a timid knock on the front door, and a young woman in her twenties would be in need of a room and a hot meal. She would follow Gabby Snow up the steep flight of stairs and Gabby would open the door to LeBarge's room and show her where to place her things, tell her to feel at home, and don't be shy to ask if you need anything. A new chapter, a new boarder, and so it goes.

But that knock had not yet sounded. Instead Caleb came clomping up the stairs. "Grandma?" his voice still carrying a slice of young boy hidden beneath its deepening tone.

"Up here, Caleb. Cleaning upstairs today."

"I finished up my chores. You said if I finished with the wood and the garden I could take care of that business I mentioned."

"Yes, about that business…what exactly does it entail?"

"Nothing much. Just something between me and LeBarge. You know…man business."

"Oh, I guess I wouldn't know much about that then. Yes, go take care of your business. When will you be home?"

"In time for dinner, of course. I'm not missing meatloaf and potatoes." Caleb removed his cap and kissed his grandmother on her cheek before taking off down the steps with all the exuberance of the young, as if he was ready to take off for flight with nothing but sheer energy fueling him. Gabby moved to the front window which overlooked the walkway to the street. Caleb came into sight with a wheelbarrow, and a bunch of tools—a shovel and pick among them and a burlap bag. In his hand was a piece of paper, folded neatly into a square that Caleb opened and studied before folding it up and placing it safely into his front pocket.

"Jerome," Gabby said aloud as there was a knock at the door.

Afterward

The Confession

LeBarge's confession was received on October 20, 1903 in a red wax-sealed envelope with the inscription:

To be sent unopened to the postmaster at Eddyville, Iowa, after my death.

"The crisis came one night while we were camping about a mile northeast of a little town called Eddyville, Iowa. Our camp was pitched in a lonesome place, under a couple of small oaks in the turn of the road. The nearest house was half a mile east, while on the road south were two graveyards. There were a few passers.

As usual we were all pretty drunk and we started the inevitable game of cards. Melalley had been morose and sullen all day and was very quarrelsome. Bill was having his usual run of good luck, while Melalley was losing heavily. Finally, Melalley threw his money-belt containing all there was left of his $15,000 on the ground in front of him, staking it all on his hand. When he called, he threw down four kings; Bill had a straight. Melalley accused Bill of cheating. With an oath Bill made a drunken lunge at Melalley with his hunting knife, laying open his arm. Melalley grabbed up a wagon stake and hit Bill a terrific blow

107

just back of the left ear. He fell like an ox. I sprang to stop them but Bill didn't budge. A hurried examination revealed his skull crushed. He gasped several times and was dead.

The horror of the crime sobered us. Gunton now had all of Melalley's money and most of mine. We knew Gunton to be an assumed name. He never spoke of any relatives. To escape the consequences of our deed, did it become known, would be difficult. There was but one thing left to do. To hide all traces of the crime, divide the money and put all possible distance between us and this spot.

Hurriedly dragging the body back from the firelight, with a knife we ripped off his clothing. Rifling his pockets of everything that might afford a clue to his identity, I threw his garments into the campfire. Just as I finished, Melalley stepped up, holding in his hand a gruesome object: It was Gunton's head, bloody and dripping, severed from the trunk. Holding it up by the long, reddish hair, the bloated countenance, the protruding eyeballs, the sneering lips, still seemingly cursing—a horrible sight—he tossed it into the fire. Writhing and twisting, the flames gnawed and scorched off flesh and hair, destroying the surest means of identification.

A dark woods bordered the road on the west, and into it, across a small ravine, we carried the headless trunk. Hurriedly digging a four-foot hole, we jammed the body in, trampling the ground down and carefully removing all evidence of its disturbance.

Going back to the fire the nauseating stench of burning flesh, warned us that the head would be too long in burning. So stepping out into the road, I buried the head in the middle of the wagon track, depending on the passing travel to obscure all traces of its hiding place.

We then scattered our campfire over the place where the butchery had taken place, to cover all traces of blood, hitched up our team and hurriedly left the scene. By daybreak we were twenty miles from the spot, and though years have passed, the crime was never discovered."

The following letter accompanied LeBarge's above confession:

Pittsburg, PA
Mr. Postmaster,

Eddyville, Iowa:—Three days ago, there died at my house in this city, Mr. Jerome LeBarge, a man with a checkered and turbulent career. He came to my house four months ago in very feeble health. He seemed to have no friends or relatives but he always paid his board regularly.

Something seemed to prey heavily on his mind. What it was he never told, but he would often start up from a sound sleep, the cold sweat breaking from every pore, seemingly trying to escape some awful influence that was stifling him.

He died in a perfect frenzy of convulsions, begging for mercy and screaming with horror of some unseen thing. It was horrible.

His secret died with him unless this packet which he made me promise to send unopened, to the postmaster at Eddyville, Iowa, contains the key.

In fulfillment of his last request, I ask you to see to it that his dying wishes, if not unreasonable, be respected.

Very truly,
Mrs. Jas. Snow.

The Gold Digger's Confession

According to *Tales of Old Eddyville*, by Frank D. Brown, W.W. DeLong, who was publisher of *The Eddyville Tribune* in 1903, at the time of LeBarge's death and confession, wrote:

> *While we do not vouch for the truthfulness of the above story, we present it as we received it, giving all the essential details of the crime—much of it condensed. The verbiage and writing of the confession shows the writer to be fairly educated, and the wording of many parts of it, convinced us that he was a close student of sensational literature, from which he absorbed many phrases which go to make up a confession. There are, however, many things regarding the matter that are convincing of its truthfulness. The one point most convincing to us is the map which accompanies the confession (which we intended to present to our readers in this issue but owing to the sickness of the editor the greater part of the week prevented him from engraving it in time for this issue).*
>
> *This map shows the place of the crime, (which our readers will readily recognize by the description) as it was 25 years ago. The trees under which the crime was alleged to have been committed, are exactly as shown on the map, only grown to large trees. The fences are shown as rail fences which are now replaced by wire. The Wylie pasture is shown as a brush pasture, which is now a cornfield, and everything excepting the natural changes that would occur in 25 years, is of remarkable accuracy. The points and distances where the body and head is buried is accurately shown although having insufficient details to easily locate them.*
>
> *The request of LeBarge is that the remains of the murdered man be given a Christian burial, as he pleads that he cannot rest*

*until it is done, and if the story is a fact, we are quite firmly con-
vinced that this has already been done by parties by LeBarge and
he makes this confession to be doubly sure that it will be done.*

*Our reason for believing this to be the case is, that in company
with several others we have carefully examined the ground and
measured the distances given by the map. Within a few feet from
where the body should be located, we found five oblong depres-
sions in the ground, two by four feet or five feet which were from
four to six inches below the surface, and looking as if several
holes had been dug, prospecting for a body or something of that
size. They are several years old, as they are sod grown and filled
with roots of the surrounding trees.*

*We will endeavor to publish the map in our next issue, and
any further details we may receive. In the meantime, a facsimile
of the map will be on exhibition at the post office news stand,
for those who desire to see it."*

Brown also noted in his *Tales of Old Eddyville*:

*The next issue, containing the map, has been ripped out of the
1903 newspaper files, possibly one of the half-dozen or more
treasure hunters from as far away as New Mexico that call at
the Tribune each year to search for clues in the files as to the location of the hidden $45,000 (probably worth over $100,000
today).*

*To add convincingly to the truthfulness of the story, a skull
was found in the approximate location in the road by road con-
struction workers in 1920. Those on the scene report a Des
Moines lady reporter took the skull promising to return it at a
later date. It was never returned.*

The Gold Digger's Confession

www.ingramcontent.com/pod-product-compliance
Lightning Source LLC
Chambersburg PA
CBHW050533280326
41933CB00011B/1568